Stoicism Leadership Principles

Lessons from Marcus Aurelius, Seneca and Stoic Philosophy to Become a Better Leader

By
Carter Mitchell

Table of Contents

Introduction

Everyone seeks to learn lessons from the past. After all, the best way to get ahead in life is to simply learn what others figured out eons ago and avoid the mistakes they made. This way, one can stand on the shoulders of giants, so to speak. Those who seek lessons from history often stumble upon the philosophy of Stoicism.

The dictionary defines a Stoic as someone who can endure pain and hardship without complaint. The word itself has a solid quality to it, and many of us use it in common language without fully appreciating the meaning of the word. Far from being a philosophy, Stoicism is a way of life.

Is it the best way of living life? Well, this is up for debate, and I will not be so arrogant as to claim that this is the solution to all the problems in the world. However, adopting a Stoic viewpoint of things does help view them with better perspective. Ultimately, it all comes down to what we think we're doing on this rock floating through space.

Often, it is extremely easy to get carried away with the ins and outs of our daily routines and we forget that there are things larger than ourselves. We're not alone in recognizing such realities. At some point, every single human society has pondered over its place in the overall scheme of things and has designed a field of philosophy to help answer some of life's most pressing questions.

The most important and pressing question is often: what is the purpose of my life? The answer to that question is often the defining characteristic of various schools of thought.

Thinking About Thought

Philosophy often turns into incomprehensible text, much like the headline of this section, which I must apologize for. I'm merely trying to make a point. It is easy to twist yourself thinking about the nature of human existence and miss many fundamental aspects of it. One can try to completely deny the negative aspects of it, one can try to sneer at life and its happenings, one can be equanimous to it, and so on.

There is no shortage of philosophies when it comes to figuring out how to live your life. No matter which philosophy you adopt, the ultimate criterion is whether it fits you well or not. This is where Stoicism fares well.

On the surface, Stoicism has an extremely negative look on the grand scheme of things. Despair and resignation blight it. Indeed, one of the men whose names graces the subtitle of this book, Seneca, was almost comically luckless throughout his life and spent his days like a leaf being battered in the high winds between one tyrant and another.

While Seneca spent most of his time ensuring his head was still attached to the rest of him, Marcus Aurelius suffered no such problems. The catch was that Marcus Aurelius suffered problems of a magnitude Seneca would have wished he had. After all, it was no easy task being the Roman emperor in charge of repairing a kingdom while dealing with an incompetent son who was busy eyeing his sister the whole time (if the movie Gladiator is to be believed).

Jokes apart, both men faced extremely different circumstances in class, life conditions, and situations, and yet turned to the same philosophy to receive answers. In addition to these two, we also have the stirring entry of Epictetus, born a slave and died a largely anonymous philosopher who is only popular these days thanks to the efforts of his student, Arrian, who took notes in class.

These three are a peculiar bunch: an opportunistic politician, an emperor, and a slave. The only thing common in their worlds was that something was always going wrong with it, which can be said of all of our lives. All three of them figured out that it wasn't the chase after good times that determines the quality of our lives, but the method of handling the bad times that contains the key to peace.

Goals and Purpose

All ancient schools of philosophy were concerned with the aim of life and how to go about living it well. Almost all of them agreed that virtue was something worthy to aim for. Almost all of them equally disagreed on how to go about achieving this. This is an interesting contrast to ancient Eastern philosophy, which talks about the same things in very different languages. Perhaps they just didn't like arguing as much in the East, who knows?

Either way, there's no dearth of opinion on how to live a good life. Neither is there any lack of material on what constitutes good leadership. Modern principles of leadership are numerous, but there's something about ancient wisdom that keeps drawing us back to it. Perhaps the fact that these principles have stood the test of time has something to do with it.

Either way, my point is that I present Stoicism not as a cure for all the ills of your life, but as a point of view which will help you lead a better one. You will find that some principles suit you while some will sound like complete nonsense. This is perfectly fine. As you will see throughout this book, our shining examples will adopt this same attitude.

The best attitude to assume as you read this book is one of open-minded curiosity. There are lessons here to emulate and mistakes to avoid. Who knows, some of the lessons might lead you to making a mistake. After all, nothing is certain. In such moments, will you use the principles of this book to deal with your disappointment? Or will you fire off an angry email castigating me as the most useless writer ever?

Well, the answer to this sort of question is also the ultimate aim of this book. As you read about the history of Stoicism, its principles, and its shining stars, keep in mind that alternate viewpoints did and do exist. I'll do my best to portray these as objectively as possible. However, a book about Stoicism can hardly be expected to give a thorough account of the ins and outs of Epicureanism.

Some of the lessons of this book might not be applicable to you because my aim is to illustrate the broad applications of Stoic thought. Instead of seeking specific advice, try to grasp the fundamental thought process behind the philosophy.

Stoicism is an invaluable tool in helping you figure out life's problems. I'm positive it will help you as much as it has helped me. So, without further ado, let's jump in and go right back to where it all began.

Chapter 1: What is Stoicism?

Throughout the ages, no matter which civilization has prospered or which political climate has persisted, there is one thing that has been common at all times, everywhere: human beings have problems. Given the nature and power of our minds, we have the ability to bring both our dreams and our nightmares into reality. A quick glance around you will show the truth of this statement.

We're surrounded by amazing creations that are born from the ingenuity of the human mind but are equally surrounded by the sort of things only a madman can dream of. The human mind is therefore a double-edged sword. Often, and history bears this out, the average human being is akin to an untrained amoeba wielding the world's most powerful tool.

Is it any surprise then that when this tool turns against us, thanks to our own machinations, we receive severe injury? Learning how to handle one's own mind is a task that has taken up a lot of time, and the thinkers and ponderers over the years have left many different blueprints.

All of these blueprints agree and say pretty much the same things, but there's a tendency to complicate matters with a lot of these methods. The human mind loves complicated stuff since it provides it with an opportunity to really stretch its legs. If complications aren't present, you can be sure the first thing the mind does is introduce it needlessly.

Hence, we have philosophical tomes which talk about talking and think about thinking and meditate on practicality. This is how we end up with philosophical doctrines that state nothing matters, so why even bother doing anything? And if nothing matters, no one matters, and therefore everything is nothing, and on and on it goes.

Stoicism is none of these things.

A Framework

Despite being a philosophy, the biggest quality Stoicism can claim for itself is just how practical it is. Stoic philosophy is not the place you look if you really want to exercise your mind with regards to deep philosophical thought. There are benefits of indulging in such thought, but Stoicism doesn't concern itself with any of that. While philosophy is a largely academic exercise, Stoicism is a practical one.

This is an important quality to note because Stoicism is not worth much unless it is put into practice. Unlike other philosophical thought, Stoicism is not concerned with what you think but more with what you do and how you behave. This emphasis on action and application is what sets it apart from other ancient philosophical thought processes.

The emphasis on action and practical advice also makes it the most accessible philosophy for someone who is facing problems in their life. Witness the fact that people from the diverse life situations of the three men highlighted in the introduction all found solace in its processes. It's not just the Ancient Romans, either.

The founding fathers are noted Stoics, and people such as the noted economist Adam Smith to the Prussian king, Frederick the Great, adopted Stoic principles to govern their lives. Even the existentialist utopia that is France has Montaigne contributing to the Stoic ranks.

Stoicism has stood the test of time, and its adoption by people from diverse backgrounds indicates the value it contains.

A Tool

The best way to think of Stoicism is to think of it as being a tool to improve your life. Much like you would use a chisel to carve a beautiful statue out of a block of marble, Stoicism has the ability to make your life better. Now, I'm not saying that you'll achieve everything you want or that your life is suddenly going to become a bed of roses.

As we'll soon see, this sort of thinking is what causes problems in the first place. Achieving alignment with reality is what Stoicism is mostly concerned with and it doesn't bother pondering over what reality is. Reality is what happens to you after all. There's no denying it, and seeking to run away from something that happened is to try to avoid life.

Aside from the improvements Stoicism can bring about in our personal lives, it has wide applications to other fields as well. Stoic principles will help you become better at whatever it is you do for a living and will enhance the quality of your relationships immeasurably. So, why is this? What exactly is the magic that Stoicism weaves that enables such massive changes in our lives?

The primary thought process on which Stoic thought relies on is the principle of inversion. Interestingly, it was the French mathematician Jacobi who was the first to give it this name ("Jacobi inversion problem," 2019). Inversion is simply the process of turning a problem on its head. Instead of asking "what should I do?", ask yourself, "what should I *not* do?" Jacobi borrowed this life principle from algebra, which he was quite adept at.

Though the Stoics never gave their thought processes such a name, inversion is omnipresent in Stoicism. This is why the philosophy seems to be such a negative one. However, to focus on just the written bits of Stoic thought is to miss the point. Interestingly, Buddhism suffers from the same misperception.

Buddha's writings are filled with treatises on misery, the root causes of it, and how one can avoid it. To read this is to think that human beings live in some special circle of hell and that happiness can never be achieved. Stoic texts read the same way. Although they are more upbeat and positive than the Buddhist texts and not as nihilistic-sounding as Taoist texts, merely reading Stoic works can convince a person that life just doesn't seem all that great.

Let's look at an example to understand the problem with this approach. If you're sick, you visit the doctor and she'll conduct a bunch of tests on you. Blood tests, ECG, you name it. The material contained in these reports is not going to paint the healthiest picture. Even if you are an athlete, you're not going to be 100% healthy at all times. If anything, a professional athlete is going to have more wrong with them thanks to injuries and such.

Either way, these reports make for not so great reading. What follows the reading of these reports though? The doctor will prescribe some course of action to make things better. If you carry out these actions, your life becomes a bit easier and soon you're out and about as if nothing happened. Don't follow these prescriptions and you'll continue to suffer.

Hence, the meditations on suffering that the Stoics write about can be seen as a doctor's report on life. Drawing conclusions from just these reports is likely to convince you that it's a miracle you're still alive. Without action, there is no point in reading them. The importance that Stoicism places on action is what makes it so effective. Much like Buddhism, there is a diagnosis and a prescription. Unfortunately, we get stuck at the diagnosis part and ignore the rest.

Versus Other Philosophies

How does Stoic thought stack up against other philosophical thought? To be brutally honest, Stoic thought is like a lightweight off the street going up against modern philosophy's Ali in his prime. Academically speaking, there isn't much to ponder over. The emphasis on action strips all possibility of deep thought.

This is not to say that Stoicism doesn't require deep meditation over its principles. I merely mean to say that you're unlikely to find modern philosophical academics deeply discussing anything to do with Stoicism since there isn't much complexity to the whole philosophy. I'm not trying to undermine academia here, just stating a fact.

There is a benefit to deep philosophical thought since it gets to the root causes of why things happen the way they do. Stoic thought begins with the assumption that things just happen and now you have to handle it. Thus, in the chain of events that lead from the root cause to the end result, Stoicism places itself pretty far down the line.

This is a natural consequence of prioritizing action over thought. I want to point out that not taking action is also a form of action, and Stoicism concerns itself with this aspect as well. Given this point of view, Stoic thought and academic philosophy exist in different worlds. While one is practical, the other is far more concerned with the "why" of things.

I'm mentioning all of this because there is an unfortunate tendency amongst some commentators to dismiss all other philosophy in favor of Stoicism. This is a bit like saying only deeply artistic indie films have value and that the latest adventures of Thor are meaningless. This is an extremely ignorant statement to make and is in fact the polar opposite of what a Stoic would say.

So, don't be so quick to dismiss all other forms of philosophy in favor of Stoicism. While there's no denying the massive benefits of practicing Stoicism in your life, understand that nothing is perfect and that all other forms of thought exist for a reason. Learning Stoicism does not require you to place blinders over your eyes or adopt a fundamentalist view of Stoicism like some modern commentators tend to.

I've been listing all of the great things about Stoicism thus far, and this is the first section where I've hinted at the fact that things are not all sunshine and cool breezes. Stoicism does have its weaknesses, and you would be remiss to not educate yourself on them. Let's take a look at these now.

Weaknesses

Before getting into the weaknesses, I'd like to point out that a difference exists between the capital "S" Stoic philosophy and the lowercase "s" stoic attitude, which is the stiff upper lip that Victorian England popularized. The latter is a subset of the former, and critiques of Stoicism often tend to confine themselves to merely the lowercase "s" version and ignore the larger picture of the philosophy.

This much is true: the lowercase "s" version provides a pretty good summary of what Stoicism is all about. Remaining unmoved despite the vicissitudes of fate and placing logic over emotions to the extent of shaming emotional outbursts are consequences of extremely Stoic thought (capital "S"). Interestingly, the British managed to popularize this to the point of caricature during their world conquest phase right when other influential forms of philosophy, such as those proposed by Kant and Schopenauer, were coming to the forefront.

These historical events actually provide a good read on the problems associated with Stoicism. Despite the stiff upper lip working for the British when it came to expanding their empire, you would have thought that the rest of continental Europe would have adopted the same attitude or, at the very least, some philosopher or academic would have drawn parallels from Ancient Greece and Rome to this sort of behavior.

Yet, there aren't any popular accounts of this happening, and the behavior was simply painted as being "British" and everyone moved on. So, why did this happen? Well, the simplest explanation is that human beings are a product of their environment and the tools we come up with enable us to deal with what is around us.

The Victorian era was a hugely prosperous time, not just for Britain, but for the rest of Western Europe as well. During this time, there were societies which once thought that the world was flat and that giant mice existed beyond the edges, exploring and conquering lands whose names they couldn't pronounce. Leaving aside the negative consequences of these actions, such as the white man's burden and so on, one must admit that these were prosperous and exciting times to be a Western European.

In such times, where hope and prosperity seemed accessible (no matter what Dickens thought of it all), what was the need to ponder on the problems occurring in life? Where was the need to sit down and think about how to best deal with problems that seemingly stemmed from uncontrollable sources? Sure, problems occurred, but there was ample hope floating around as well, in the form of the promise of prosperity. In short, the environment was one of positive change.

In contrast to this, we have the lives and times of our three famous Stoic philosophers. Epictetus was born a slave, so his beginnings need no description of the horrors he would have faced and witnessed around him. Seneca was a politician during not just one madman's reign but two, the latter being the one who ordered him to commit suicide. Marcus Aurelius presided over the rebuilding of a broken empire, and while he was the last of the line of great kings who achieved this, surely he must have seen that the writing was on the wall for the Western Roman Empire.

In short, all of our heroes lived through exceedingly bleak times. For all of its prosperity, Roman society was barbarous at the best of times. During Seneca's time, it was routine for pregnant women to be thrown to wild animals in arenas (Aptowicz, 2019). Essentially, the Romans during this time took regular levels of insanity and cranked it all the way up to ten.

What was a sensible man to do in the middle of all of this? The rise of Stoicism, as we'll see in a later chapter, is also marked by an imbalance of power in Ancient Greece. At every step and high point of Stoic thought, when we dig deeper, we see that a lack of stability and increasing randomness in the lives of those proposing it is common.

Thus, we can surmise that Stoic philosophy is ideally suited for bleak times or for those who are going through extremely tough times in their lives. There is no denying the usefulness of it. To adopt this view during prosperous times might be a bit too much though. Mind you, this is merely my point of view. Stoicism has prescriptions for happy times as well, but when studying these you must keep this background information in mind to make an informed decision and avoid a fundamentalist view of Stoicism.

Is this why Stoicism as a philosophy has seen a resurgence in the West? You'd be hard pressed to find an Indian or Chinese person who agrees with these points of view. While the fact that those countries have ample ancient philosophical material of their own to draw from might be a factor in this, there is no denying that the overall picture in those countries is very similar to what existed in Western Europe on the cusp of the industrial revolution (Anil, 2017).

This brings me to the next weakness of Stoicism. It is essentially a philosophy that is grounded in Western principles. I'm using the word "Western" here to indicate the influence of Ancient Greek and Roman societies. Our modern forms of government, law and politics all draw inspiration from here, and it can be easy to assume that these principles are the only valid ones thanks to their hegemony. This is just simple human psychology—whatever you experience through your senses is what will have the greatest validity in your mind.

However, Stoic thought assumes a lot of things that are incompatible with a non-Western mode of thought and ethics. While the broad strokes of Stoic thought would fit very well in any society, the deeper you go into the rabbit hole, the greater the bias you are adopting in your thinking.

I'll illustrate this with an example. The highest goal that the Ancient Greeks established for themselves was Eudaimonia, which is a fancy word to describe a good life filled with happiness and contentment. A life well-lived, in other words. Contrast this to ancient subcontinental (the Indian subcontinent, as distinct from the modern country of India) aim of attaining *Moksha*, which is a good death.

Both philosophies are broadly concerned with achieving a good life, but their means to get there are completely different. The inherent biases are wildly different. This is not meant to be a debate about which is better than the other. Such decisions are personal choices. My point is that reacting in a deeply Stoic manner and acting on biases inherent in such thoughts in an average subcontinental setting is not going to decrease your misery. If anything, it's going to compound it.

Lastly, I'd like to highlight Stoicism's views on the primacy of logic over emotion. Again, viewing this from the prism of the events that precipitate such views helps us understand why adopting this viewpoint might result in less than ideal results for you. In a world which is deeply unstable and where people aren't quite sure what is going to come next, there is a tendency to react irrationally to events.

Think of it this way: if you knew you were going to die tomorrow for sure, what would you do right now? Odds are that your current task, no matter how important or rational it might be, is not going to rate very high in the overall scheme of things. Humans are emotional creatures, and to somehow insinuate that emotions are invalid is to adopt an extreme view of things.

The fact is that we cannot process everything logically, and a lot of decisions are driven by intuition and feeling. To suppress this is to lose a portion of yourself, a bit like deliberately not using your non-dominant hand for tasks since you reason it isn't as strong as your other one. To do this is to miss the point of having two hands completely.

I'm not saying that Stoicism says all emotions are invalid. This is a myth that I'll clear up in another chapter. My point is that there is a tendency to want to apply rationality to every single thing in your life, and to live this way is to live a miserable life. The aim of Stoicism is to ease suffering, not provide happiness.

There's a small but significant difference between the two approaches, and if you understand the environment that Stoicism thrives in, it makes sense of why this is. In times of instability, the best plan of action is to cut out distractions or reduce them to the barest minimum and make informed decisions. Hence, we have the minimization of emotion. Doing this at all times makes no sense.

So, when you read this book, do keep all of these points in mind. You've probably picked this book up because you've read some new age entrepreneur raving about how Stoicism helped them build their business or some such nonsense. It wasn't Stoicism that helped them create it, that was done thanks to their own creative abilities.

Stoicism helps you deal with tough moments and helps you make informed decisions in such times. In short, it helps you make things less bad. It's like a shovel that helps you fill up a hole you've dug by mistake and stumbled into.

It is not a magic bullet but simply a tool. Make it a part of your toolbox and understand when to use it and when to shelve it.

Chapter 2: Who is a Stoic?

On the surface of it, this is a simple question to answer. A Stoic is someone who practices Stoicism. Simple. However, this isn't a philosophical book for nothing! No, we're going to dig deeper into the meaning of that question and see if we can learn more about Stoicism by examining the practices and habits of someone who professes to be one.

The first thing to point out is that, as you read in the previous chapter, Stoicism applies to anyone from any walk of life. More importantly, it is of the greatest help when things are going poorly and is designed to help you make things less bad, but its aim isn't to make you happy.

Understanding the differences between those points of view is critical for you to truly understand what Stoicism is all about. Having said that, let's look at who a Stoic really is.

Practices

As I mentioned earlier, the greatest mark of a Stoic is their ability to focus on practice and action. Stoicism might have a bunch of principles with fancy names, but it all hinges on how well you can practice them in life. All the teachings and tenets of the philosophy ultimately point back to this one truth.

So really, a Stoic is defined by his or her emphasis on carrying out and living some basic principles. Such principles can be immensely rewarding when dealing with the troublesome areas of life. All of these principles can be described as being defensively pessimistic. Now, the law of attraction crowd might think of all this as being counter to happiness, but the truth is that by working out the worst-case scenarios of things and by having no expectations, you actually reduce the burden on yourself.

So, let's look at some common habits of both modern and ancient Stoics.

Misfortune

I'll begin with the most pessimistic view of things right off that bat. This practice was a favorite of Seneca's since his life was absurdly unstable with one seemingly good thing only leading to something worse. I don't mean to say that our hero suffered on a daily basis, but his life can hardly be said to be a stable or a conventionally happy one.

Seneca's advice was to practice misfortune in your daily life, especially when something good happens to you. By doing this, according to him, you'll be steeling yourself for the inevitably bad stuff that will occur. If it doesn't, well you're still well off. In short, being prepared is what life is all about, and you ought to be very cautious about your frame of mind when experiencing the joy of success.

One method of doing this, as per Seneca, was to practice poverty. Some of you might chuckle that you don't need any practice at that! Well, whatever your station is, try living at a level below it. Deny yourself the good things you have for a week and practice living as someone who doesn't have the things you take for granted.

How about eating three square meals a day? Get by with two. Set yourself a budget which is absurdly lower than what you usually spend and live on that. This practice has a lot of benefits to it since it gets you to appreciate the good things in your life. Comfort and the comfort zone are our biggest enemies since they prevent us from expanding our lives.

I'm not saying this method is going to get you to expand, but by reminding yourself of the negative, you're making yourself aware of the existence of the positive. A lot of Stoic thought functions along these lines.

Good Versus Bad

Stoic thought proposes that there is no such thing as good or bad. They might exist in some small degree, but what drives them to take up large parts of emotional space in our minds is our perception of them. This is another way of saying that things happen. It is our reaction to it that makes them good or bad.

When it comes to living life, this is a far more realistic and practical approach to handling problems than the Panglossian attitude that everything happens for the best ("Pangloss-character," 2006). Ironically, by adopting an indifferent view to things, you will become living proof that everything does happen for the best. This tenet is a prime example of the practice of inversion in action.

Stoics advocate turning a problem on its head to view it as an opportunity instead. In the words of Marcus Aurelius, "the obstacle is the way," (Oppong, 2017). If you've put a lot of effort into building something and it comes crashing down instead, this isn't a moment to identify with sadness and disappointment. Instead, it is a prime opportunity for you to practice your ability to bounce back and deal with sadness.

By reframing things in this manner, to the opposite side of things, you'll increase your ability to turn things in your favor. It is small wonder then that a lot of new age entrepreneurs favor Stoicism.

Think about the difficulties of running a new business. Things keep crashing down even when they're going well. There's a lot of uncertainty and the stress can be overwhelming. The practice of inversion helps people deal with this stress and actually turns obstacles into opportunities. This is how a lot of great products are born.

In order to progress forward and outside your comfort zone, you need to deal with obstacles. A practicing Stoic knows this very well. Hence, figuring out the best attitude to take toward obstacles is of utmost importance. Once you prepare your mind to think about obstacles in a helpful manner, the solution will present itself.

Dust to Dust

According to Marcus Aurelius, Alexander conquered ungodly portions of the world. He commanded legions of armies and managed to stitch together an empire that was as diverse as the world at that time had ever seen. However, in death he was no different from the guy who drove his mule (Oppong, 2017).

Perhaps this was Marcus' method of reminding himself of his own mortality and his importance in the overall scheme of things, who knows? Ultimately, the lesson from this story is clear: A Stoic is well aware of how small and insignificant their achievements and thoughts really are in the long run.

Another one of Aurelius' practices provides more insight into this. He used to make it a habit of listing out all those people who annoyed him, those whom he felt anger toward, those who felt anger toward him, and so on. How many of those emotions really meant anything in the overall scheme of things?

The Ancient Greeks were obsessed with the topic of patheiai, which roughly translates to passion in modern English. However, this is not a true translation. The Greek word symbolizes irrational behavior and actions that are born out of impulse, without concern for consequences.

Passion (the Greek version) overtakes us at all moments in our lives. How much energy have you wasted raging at the person who cut you off in traffic? What did it really matter to you in the larger scheme of things? Not much, probably. Does this mean you shouldn't care about anything? Does anything even matter? Well, not quite.

The idea is that one needs to be concerned but not get overly attached to the events around them. Yes, they're real and they affect you, but what is of utmost importance is doing the right thing at a particular moment and not being overly concerned about what might be said about you or what people might think of you. What is truly important? Your respect for a life well led, or the satisfaction of someone outside of yourself? The answer is obvious.

The Bird's Eye View

Something that helps you get outside of yourself and view things as they're meant to be is to take the bird's eye view of things. Marcus refers to this as Plato's view. As an aside, this is a key aspect of Stoicism. It's ability to filter the best from different schools of thought is what has made it so robust. After all, Plato was a Sophist, not a Stoic.

Either way, taking the bird's eye view achieves twin objectives. The first is that it reminds you of your own place in the grand scheme of things. Let's look at this from Marcus Aurelius' point of view. Here is the most powerful man in the known world, and as he zooms out above Rome, he sees masses of people who are under his rule. As he goes further out, he encounters the first bunch of people who don't think too much of him.

The further out he goes, the greater the number of people he sees, and soon he sees cultures which he has no clue about. Neither do those teeming masses of people have any idea who he is or what he even looks like. Soon, he's viewing the entire globe and Rome isn't even a speck, and he himself is but a mite of dust. In consideration of all this, what does it matter that the slave girl misplaced his favorite pair of socks?

The other insight you will receive from this is to recognize the interdependence of human beings on one another. Nothing is possible in this world without the support of both like-minded people and those opposed to you. The ones opposed to you provide you with ideal obstacles to overcome and are valuable when it comes to moving past your comfort zone. Viewed in this manner, you owe it to those around you to give back to them and do your best in helping them live better lives.

The interdependence of humanity was something the Stoics were deeply conscious about, and taking a holistic approach to things was what the bird's eye view achieved for them.

Memento Mori

I'll discuss this in far greater theoretical detail later, but for now understand that this practice literally means meditating on your own mortality. This is perfectly in line with the other practices we've looked at thus far. Unsurprisingly, this practice comes from Seneca, for whom death could literally have come at any second.

Seneca advises to behave and act as if life could end at this very second. The act of reflecting on how life could end might seem pessimistic, but this is missing the point. If anything, it frees you to do things and to reflect on your actions on a deeper level. If you were to die right now, how would you want to be remembered? Would you yell and lash out at someone who angers you if you were to die right after this moment?

Marcus Aurelius found solace in this practice as well. He also advises us to act as if life could leave us at any second (Robertson, 2018). With this thought in mind, act accordingly. Of course, the Stoics' point is that a life of virtue is the highest goal and that this is how you ought to live. I'm mentioning this in case you misinterpret this practice to mean that you ought to head over to Vegas and try your luck at the tables this instant.

A Stoic thus believes that life needs to be lived to the fullest and only in pursuit of those things that are truly worthwhile. Spending time on things that do not matter is the biggest waste of time there is since time is precisely what could be snatched away at any instant.

Control What You Can

A lot of things are going to happen to you. How many of these things can you really control? You want to travel somewhere but there's a storm and you now you can't get out of the house. Or perhaps your home has been blown away and you can kiss any trips goodbye for the next few years. What can you control?

The truth is that when people react, we tend to react mostly to the stuff we cannot control. These are the things we constantly rail against and worry about. You cannot control what The Donald is going to tweet. So, what is the point in worrying about which way the country is going to go? You can control what your action in this and the next moment is going to be. Thus, control that instead.

This goes back to the point of things happening and determining your reaction to it. Doing so is literally worrying about things that happened in the past and that moment has gone. So, why worry about it? React and live in the present and solve what's in front of you. The rest will fall wherever it falls. You don't control that.

More than anything else, it is this habit that defines a Stoic. Reflecting on this question constantly and in every situation will help you separate the important from the unimportant and will inform you of what action you need to take. This and the previous point tie in very closely with the Buddhist principle of letting go of the need for an "I."

The "I" is your ego, and this is what causes suffering and is constantly reacting to the things you cannot control since it needs fuel to develop an identity. The identity is what creates contrast and gives it meaning. Stoic philosophy contends that everything is connected, so where is the notion of a separate identity in all of this?

Journaling

Epictetus was of the opinion that philosophy is "written down day by day" and that this was how his students ought to "exercise themselves" (Robertson, 2018). All three major pillars of Stoicism did it, with Seneca mentioning that the sleep which followed his journaling habit was the sweetest of all (Robertson, 2018). Marcus Aurelius' journals are some of the most treasured texts, not just in Stoicism, but in all of literature itself.

The Stoic practice of journaling goes beyond the "dear diary" method of teenage girls. Ideally, your journaling ought to be structured in a certain manner so that you can examine your day and reflect on what you did well, what you learned, and where you can improve. This doesn't mean to say that it needs to be dull as ditchwater. The idea is to engage your mind to improve and to hold yourself to a high standard.

The practice of writing before bed also helps relieve the frustrations of the day and helps iron out any lingering problems, as research has shown (Robertson, 2018). The ancient Stoics didn't have access to this research but intuitively knew that the practice has its benefits.

Make journaling a part of your day's end and you'll see the benefit every practicing Stoic sees in their lives. One thing I'd like to point out here is that the act of journaling is not a practice. It is Stoicism itself, as Epictetus mentions. To practice and to be a Stoic are one and the same thing.

What's the Worst That Could Happen?

This practice refers to the tenet of premeditatio malorum, or the act of visualizing everything that could go wrong. Note that this is not expecting things to go wrong but simply visualizing it as a tool to be prepared in advance. This thin line is what separates Stoicism from outright pessimism.

As Seneca wrote in one of his letters, nothing unexpected ever happens to the wise man. This doesn't mean to say that you should work out all the permutations and combinations of things that could go wrong. It's just that you should keep in mind that there is a possibility that you will not receive the benefits you deserve.

This is truth in life since life itself is chaotic. Our minds are not evolved enough to figure out patterns in the scheme of things. Instead of trying to make sense of chaos, simply assume that it will happen and focus instead of preparing yourself for it. In this manner, you're prepared ahead of time should unfavorable things come to pass.

This exercise builds your resilience and mental strength and will affirm to you that no matter what happens, you will move forward and you will thrive. The expectation of thriving is not a part of Stoic philosophy but is rather what will occur as a result. Stoic thought is not too concerned with the exact nature of results as long as it means that your mind is well prepared and in the perfect frame for dealing with the randomness that is inherent to life.

Amor Fati

Our minds have a built-in negative bias that causes us to look at what is wrong before arriving at what is right. Think about your relationships with your loved ones. While you care about them and love them, often you'll find yourself ruminating on what's wrong with them. It is a fundamental truth of our existence that the more time we spend with someone, the more we focus on their faults.

Well, our life is something we spend the most time with, if that makes sense. Amor fati, which translates to "a love of fate," implies that loving everything that happens is the best way to live since acceptance of life as it is is crucial for happiness. Wondering about stuff that isn't there or wishing that something else would happen is for fools since there isn't anything you can do about it.

Of course, you can work toward an ideal goal, but pursuing a goal because of its absence is different from pursuing it to realize its presence. Like everything else with Stoicism, there is a subtle difference in perspective that changes the way you view things. As Epictetus said, wish for things to happen the way they happen and, in this way, you'll always get what you want.

A lot of people have trouble wrapping their heads around this idea. Does this mean you should wish for bad things to happen? Well, there is no good or bad, remember? Everything is an opportunity to grow, and the idea of amor fati is simply a consequence of this line of thought.

Be in love with whatever happens in your life even if it seems unbearable. Adopt Plato's view and see them for what they really are. Above all else, don't just talk about Stoicism; embody it. To be a Stoic is to practice its principles all the time and to keep working on improving your practice. Ultimately, this is the greatest virtue.

Where does this emphasis on virtue come from and what is its connection to happiness? Stoicism seems to draw and share commonalities with a lot of different areas of philosophy, so how did all this come about? Well, this is what we'll look at next.

Chapter 3: The History of Stoicism

"Why bother with the history of Stoicism?" you might be wondering. After all, if you just knew the practices and major tenets, wouldn't you be good to go? Not quite. You see, Stoic thought borrows freely from a lot of other influential philosophies that were floating around at the time, and to fully grasp the meaning of some of the things we'll be looking at later in this book, you need to understand where they first came from.

Secondly, there's always something to learn by examining the history of an idea. The environment in which an idea is born is crucial to understand how it needs to be applied. I've covered this topic in the first chapter and will reiterate my point here again. Stoicism is a great philosophy to design your life around.

However, you should never make the mistake of assuming that this is the only way of living. To do so would be to misunderstand the philosophy, ironically. So, having clarified that, let's go all the way back to when the first seeds of philosophy began to sprout.

Western Thought

Western philosophy has evolved in an environment different from that prevailing in the east. The first recognized philosopher lived in the 6th century B.C. He was named Thales and hailed from a place called Miletus ("A Quick History of Philosophy," 2019). Science as a field of study did not exist back then, so a natural blurring of subjects occurred.

We today think of philosophy and science as two distinct lines of thought, but ancient philosophy combined aspects of both along with theology and spirituality to form one big confusing mess. The emphasis a philosopher placed on a particular area of thought is what determined the distinction between philosophical schools more than anything else.

Anyway, back to Thales. He was primarily concerned with natural phenomena such as the weather, its relation to mathematics (which were rudimentary at the time), and the budding subject of physics, although he didn't think of them as being very separate. Above all else, Thales' thoughts drifted toward finding logical explanations for naturally occurring phenomena. Was it possible that lightning and thunder were not caused by Apollo but by some interaction between naturally occurring items? Also, what was man's nature in all of this? Since humans were a part of nature, didn't it follow that the elements of humanity were the same as those found in nature?

Such were his thoughts as he and his disciples wandered about staring at the clouds. Mind you all that cloud staring did have a side benefit. Thales figured out that weather patterns indicated a large bumper harvest for olives in his region and went around cornering the market on olive presses. How he did this is a great story in and of itself, but I'm not going to focus on that too much here.

Basically, Thales invented the world's first recorded call-option contract and made a ton of money which enabled him to retire and keep thinking about more stuff ("A Quick History of Philosophy," 2019). He eventually came to the conclusion that the primary element human beings were made out of was water and that this replicated itself throughout the universe.

Some of his disciples begged to differ and insisted that fire was the primary element. Yet another group insisted it was air. This meandering was put to a close by the final group, possibly the cleverest of them all, which insisted that everything was made of "the infinite." No one could argue against that, so philosophy moved on from this.

Pre- to Post-Socratic Thought

Thales' pondering is common of pre-Socratic philosophy. The philosophers during this period concerned themselves with questions dealing with nature, logic, and change. While some of their questions were directed at understanding how to deal with these things, the majority of their time was spent debating the nature of them.

Change was one such example. Heraclitus proposed that the world was a constant interplay of change, while Parmenides performed some remarkable mental gymnastics to prove that change was an illusion and that everything in this world is permanent and indestructible ("A Quick History of Philosophy," 2019).

All of this debating seems silly to us these days, but keep in mind that during this time, science simply didn't exist. Natural phenomena, such as water evaporating and pouring down from the sky, seemed miraculous. Therefore, these baby steps were as important scientifically as they were philosophically. A good example of this is the theory of atomism, proposed by Democritus, which posited that everything in the world was comprised of tiny, indestructible objects, which is what the atom was named after when discovered.

Pythagoras was another pre-Socratic philosopher who is best known for his theorem today but back then was known as the leader of a religious cult that believed the whole world was run by numbers. This cult even murdered one of its former members when he dared to expose the discovery of irrational numbers to the world, thereby challenging the underlying ethos of the cult ("A Quick History of Philosophy," 2019).

As the world meandered along into the 4th century, classical philosophy came into being through the thoughts of Socrates, Plato, and Aristotle. Socratic thought is often referred to as Sophist thought, while Plato managed to get a whole branch of philosophy, Platonism, named after himself. This trio were the first to debate the role of ethics and how it played a part in people's lives.

Common issues that were debated included the right way to live one's life and whether it was possible for a person to reason their way towards a good life. Were good and right the same thing? What would a good and right thought process be? As you can see, the focus of philosophical thought had turned inwards. From debating what was going on around them, philosophers began examining the world and how it related to people.

Plato was probably the most prolific in terms of production, taking down Socrates' notes and producing his own work. Eventually, he blended the fields of ethics, metaphysics, epistemology, and politics into one single flowing philosophy, and this moment marked the time when philosophers officially received permission to start complicating stuff.

Plato is also the first recorded philosopher to state that virtue was the highest human aim and was the key to a good life. The term *Eudaimonia* makes its first appearance around this time. Aristotle, Plato's student, took his teacher's work a step further and added the budding field of science to Plato's framework and also developed the field of syllogism. This is perhaps the most influential work in the study of logic and remained a force until the late 19th century ("A Quick History of Philosophy," 2019).

As all of this was going on, a number of schools were developing and flourishing around Ancient Greece. A lot of these schools were offshoots of the primary ones. Indeed, the majority of philosophical schools were branches of Sophism, and this is how the Cynical school of thought came to be born. Cynicism, unlike its current-day meaning, advocated a life of living as close to nature as possible in order to ensure happiness.

Self-sufficiency and the rejection of all material connections were hallmarks of this school of thought, and no one encapsulated its bizarre teachings more than Diogenes, who ate raw meat and lived in a bathtub, among other things.

The Cynics, no matter how eccentric they were, had the right ideas. It's just that they were far too fundamentalist about them to make sense. Also, Cynicism had no practical value in terms of enabling people to live life. After all, if someone was unhappy with the problems they faced, the Cynical reply that they thought the problems were a problem is hardly much of a solution (notwithstanding the inevitable insult that would have followed from the Cynic).

A man named Zeno, hailing from Citium, had the same thoughts and decided to found his own school of philosophy.

Zeno of Citium

The sheer length of the history of Stoicism is reflected in the fact that Zeno's Stoic beliefs are very different from that of later Stoics. If anything, Zeno's treatises have a lot more in common with ancient Eastern philosophy than the duty-focused philosophy common with later Stoics, which would go on to become the foundation of early Christian philosophy ("A Quick History of Philosophy," 2019).

Either way, Zeno offered what was considered to be a less extreme version of Cynicism. Lecturing and debating from a stoa, or a porch, Zeno's ideas of virtue being the highest goal to aim for and that material attraction was what caused suffering found a lot of takers. His stoa would go on to provide the name for his school of thought as well, and soon Stoicism began to gain many followers, primarily because people were fed up with the antics of the Cynics and the impracticality of the Epicureans (another school which emphasized connection with nature and seclusion).

Zeno's primary focus was on achieving detachment, much like Buddhist philosophy, but the way he went about it belied his cynical roots. His rhetoric was gruff and abrasive, and he had no qualms about mocking the rich and wealthy of Athens for their hoarding of wealth.

A lot of his principles were considered rather shocking at the time. Examples include his call to overhaul the education system (some things never change), his exhortation that only the virtuous be eligible for citizenship, that men and women be considered equal and should wear similar clothing, that so-called deviant sexual practices such as masturbation, homosexuality, and prostitution be considered normal, that free love (that is women not being treated as the possessions of men) be the new norm, and finally that all temples, courts of law, and even money be abolished since a truly virtuous citizenry would have no need for such things ("A Quick History of Philosophy," 2019).

His beliefs on nature are much the same as ancient Eastern philosophy in that the entire universe was one God and that it possesses a reasoning of its own which man cannot process. He also wove a common thread through Thales' debates with his students by stating that this divine reason was simply an æther which took on various forms, becoming air, water, fire, wind, and earth, thus giving form to the world as it is.

He also proposed that all humans belonged to a common soul, and that everything in this world went through cycles of creation and destruction and that neither could exist without the other. His death in 263 B.C. is retold in the works of his students as being an aptly philosophical one. Apparently, Zeno passed away by simply holding his breath, thereby asserting that man has full control over his own self.

Despite this being a bald-faced lie, one must admit that it makes for a great story and a fitting ending for the founder of Stoicism.

Seneca

Following Zeno's death, Stoicism continued to flourish thanks to his most prolific students, Cleanthes and Chryssipus. To study the history of Ancient Greek philosophy at this time is to also realize that as a power, Greece was continuously losing ground to Rome. What was once a thriving and dominant civilization of city states was now a ruptured network of warlords relying on former glories.

The days of Alexander running amok had long gone, and it was natural that culturally the ancient world began recognizing the two major powers in the Mediterranean: Rome and Carthage. The Punic Wars ensured that Rome remained unchallenged as the sole world power. In fact, Rome had already become a center of culture long before this time. However, by 4 B.C., the time Lucius Annaeus Seneca was born, the Western Roman Empire was busy destroying itself.

Seneca spent his youth in Rome where his father was a member of the senate. One of his teachers during his early years was a man by the name of Attalus the Stoic. As a youth, Seneca suffered from regular bouts of ill-health and retired to Egypt to recover, under the care of his influential aunt. Upon their return to Rome, thanks to his aunt's influence, Seneca secured a place as a Quaestor and entered Roman political life. From this point on, Seneca's life was one misplaced word away from being snatched from him. The first incident that enforced this truth was when the incumbent emperor, Caligula, ordered him executed because Seneca was far too good at oratory.

Funnily enough, his ill-health saved him since Caligula grew bored of torturing a sick man. Caligula eventually found his way to the great exit sign in the sky and was succeeded by Claudius. Upon ascending to the throne, he promptly decided to exile Seneca despite a false accusation being thrown at him.

Our luckless philosopher was exiled to Corsica where he produced two of his greatest works, with the second one suspiciously showering praise after praise on Claudius. Sure enough, he was soon called back to Rome as a tutor for the young Nero. This was akin to going from the frying pan into the fire as Nero proved to be an even bigger tyrant than his predecessors.

While the initial years under Nero were prosperous for Rome, the emperor eventually aged out of Seneca's influence and soon went about murdering those who offended him. Even by Ancient Roman standards this was a bit too much. The duty of justifying these deeds fell to Seneca who delivered the goods and ensured the emperor didn't have to face a senate revolt. Despite this, he was soon banished to the countryside and there Seneca published two more of his famous works.

After a botched attempt on the emperor's life, Nero ordered Seneca to commit suicide by consuming poison. His final hours are depicted as being similar to Socrates', and tended by his young wife, Seneca passed away from this world. Except he didn't. The poison didn't work completely, and he slit his wrists with the intention of bleeding out. His ill-health meant he couldn't bleed out and was transferred to a warm bath in order to assist the process. Even in death, Seneca couldn't catch a break.

The point behind this brief biography of Seneca is to illustrate the rough nature of his circumstances as well as the fact that Seneca's true motivations behind his works are not fully understood. A number of his exemplary works were produced under the threat of imminent death and one can hardly fault him for placing his own neck ahead of the need to advance global philosophy.

As it was, Seneca found the greatest peace via the adoption of Stoic principles. Seneca does concern himself with questions of natural order, but his focus is far more on the ethical and interpersonal side of things. Seneca's ultimate aim was to enable someone to find peace. As such, Zeno's focus on humans being a part of nature is relegated to the sidebar.

The theme of planning for the worst also makes sense when viewed through the prism of Seneca's life. After all, one disaster followed the next over the course of his life. It's easy to see why he viewed a person's ability to prepare themselves for the worst as being crucial for happiness.

How much of Seneca's life was the result of him being subject to forces out of his control, and how much of it was due to his own actions? There is a danger of viewing Seneca as being the collateral damage of a trio of madmen, but reality is a lot more complex than that. Despite his exhortations to virtue, there is no doubt that Seneca amassed his wealth through dubious means when in Nero's favor.

In fact, his repeated desired to return to Rome belies a need for the power that was on offer there. While this isn't a bad thing itself, we must keep this context in mind when studying anything to do with Seneca.

Epictetus

The first few years of Epictetus' life and the last few of Seneca's overlapped one another. There is no doubt that when growing up Epictetus would have heard and read Seneca's works and would have been influenced by him to a certain extent. Indeed, given the sort of tumult the Western Roman Empire was facing those days, Stoicism began to outstrip Cynicism as the dominant philosophy ("A Quick History of Philosophy," 2019).

Epictetus' parents presumably sold him into slavery as a child and, curiously enough, he was bought by one of Nero's secretaries. Not much is known of the conditions Epictetus had to endure beyond the fact that they were terrible. At one point, his master is said to have broken his leg which consigned him to being lame for the rest of his life.

Soon after Nero's death, he managed to procure his freedom and lived out a life of ill-health. He began teaching philosophy in Rome and it is here we see a divergence from Seneca. Epictetus' tone of teaching is decidedly religious, and he is the first major Stoic philosopher to emphasize the importance of duty.

This theme of duty would later be taken up by early Christianity and would find its way into the Old Testament. Around 90 A.D., he and a number of other philosophers were expelled from Rome thanks to their teachings making far too much sense, which was against the interests of the resident tyrant at the time, Domitian.

Epictetus spent the rest of his life in exile and it is during this time that his pupil, Arrian, recorded all of his teacher's sayings. This is a good thing because Epictetus himself wrote nothing of note. As opposed to Seneca, who was concerned with politics and high-level interpersonal dealings, Epictetus was far more concerned with pondering over the connections between nature and man and its implications on ethics.

In this, Epictetus closely resembles the Sophists and is different from Seneca. An example of this is the fact that Epictetus prescribes that man must believe in a higher force of God which is far more intelligent than he is. One can see the allure of this thought process to early religious thinkers.

Epictetus agreed with Seneca in that the nature of man was self-preservation but veered away from him by stating that the best method of ensuring self-preservation was to contribute to the greater good. Hence, man had a duty to contribute to his society and commonwealth (Scott, 2018).

Duty plays a major part in his writings and in this he is markedly different from the other two pillars of Stoicism (Seneca and Marcus Aurelius). As a note, I don't wish to convey the impression that these three were the only major Stoics along with Zeno. It's just that their works are the most popular due to the fact that they've survived the longest.

Stoicism as a philosophy had many takers during this time, and it was a commonly accepted mode of thought, even if modern Stoics do not conform to it in large parts.

Either way, Stoicism as a philosophy was evolving and the waypoints of Seneca, Epictetus, and Marcus highlight its versatility and longevity. Consider the fact the Zeno never used the word duty or even considered the collective as a major issue when discussing Stoic ethics. The differences in the teachings between all of the proponents of the philosophy shows how relevant Stoicism has been and still is to our lives.

For now, though, let's move onto our next philosophical titan, Marcus Aurelius.

Marcus Aurelius

Just as Seneca's late life and Epictetus' early life overlapped, so did Marcus' early years and Epictetus' old age. In contrast to the previous two, Marcus was actually born during a time of Roman prosperity. Aside from this, his father was a powerful Praetor, his mother a wealthy heiress, and his uncle was the emperor. All in all, young Marcus didn't face too many troubles at the start.

For Rome as a whole, this was the era of the Five Good Kings, which refers to a series of kings who undid the damage of the previous madmen. A state of normalcy, by Roman standards, had returned to the empire. Marcus, by the age of 17, had been anointed as a possible future emperor along with his adoptive brother Lucius Verus. Under the tutelage of their uncle Antonius Pius, both boys learned the ins and outs of government.

After the death of their uncle, which little is known about, both Marcus and Lucius ascended to the throne as co-emperors (Gill, 2019). Not much is known about Verus outside of Marcus' musings. By all accounts he was a competent politician and military strategist. Despite the prosperity Rome was enjoying outwardly, Marcus was to soon find that the empire had been maneuvered into a tough position financially.

This is not to say that Rome was poor, but that it was inflexible and relied on continued conquests to keep things going. The rest of Marcus' reign was blighted by continuous conflict, and at one point his troops managed to win the war they were waging but also brought back the plague with them which decimated Rome.

Marcus' reign is a largely confused one, and in political terms, he doesn't score too many points. Indeed, as an emperor, Marcus is often confused as being one of the greatest of them all thanks to his literary fame. His work, *Meditations*, is a compilation of his journals throughout his life, and in this he was directly influenced by the works of Epictetus.

Unlike other emperors, Marcus adopted an heir and then promptly saw the fragile balance he had maintained get shot to pieces by his successor, Commodus. Thus began the terminal decline of the Western Roman Empire, which further highlights Marcus as being a great emperor when in reality it was probably his actions that triggered the decline.

Either way, Marcus' competence as an emperor is not the point here. The point is that there is no more prolific and easily accessible author when it comes to Stoicism, and this fame manages to boost Marcus' perceived talents in other areas. As it stands, he does not offer any original philosophy of his own but stands out as a shining example of the application of Stoic principles.

All in all, the lives of these men provide a fascinating backdrop to the principles of Stoic philosophy and also inform us of how the philosophy changed. The common thread, as mentioned before, has been of upheaval. During times of uncertainty, Stoicism has been the balm that has enabled people to live their best lives, or at the very least, make sense of them.

Modern Stoicism exists in the form of dedicated online communities and has seen a resurgence thanks to Web 2.0. This should not be surprising if one considers the state of today's Western world. Opinions are at an extreme, and the landscape has changed a lot faster than ever before. Consider that the millennial generation has lived through changes in a single lifetime that once took multiple generations.

A person in their mid-thirties who grew up in the West has gone from having no internet to using a smartphone anywhere and at any time. Let's just take a second to process the enormity of that change. Back in the '80s, *The Terminator* was a sci-fi flick. These days the topic of that movie is an actual discussion between the likes of Elon Musk and Larry Page, the founders of Tesla and Google, respectively (Song, 2019).

Change is afoot, and what history teaches us is that Stoicism has a place in all of this. This is not to say that times are bad. Far from it. It's just that human beings are notoriously bad at dealing with change, and by adopting Stoic principles in our lives, perhaps we can make better sense of what is happening all around us.

Even if this fails, the mental peace we will achieve by doing this will surely be worth something in the end.

Chapter 4: The Tenets of Stoicism

Stoicism as a philosophy covers a lot of ground, and I'll be taking a look at particular topics in detail in the next chapter. Before doing that though, it is important to gather all the basic tenets of Stoicism to prepare for the more detailed dives into the philosophy.

Stoicism has changed and morphed over time, but all that has really changed over the years are the technicalities. There are variations to modern Stoicism as well, and the exact nature of these are better suited for an academic philosophical book. The truth is that the basics of Stoicism alone will take you far and will ensure a pretty good quality of life.

We've looked at some of these in the second chapter, so some of this might be repetitive. Do note though that those principles were presented with a view to applying them as practices, whereas here my concern is more theoretical and with an interest in forming a framework of ideas upon which we can expand our dive into Stoicism.

So, let's take a look at Stoicism's basic principles!

Action in Accordance with Nature

This is a common theme with ancient philosophy since the Socratics era, when the focus of investigation shifted from the world around us to the interaction of our own world with the one outside of us. Stoic philosophy proposes that in order to live one's best life, virtue is necessary. One of the main markers of virtue is the ability to live as close as possible to nature.

Note that nature here is intended to mean both the universe as well as the true nature of a human being. So, the point here is to pay attention to both what is outside as well as inside, and this isn't just about adopting a hippie-like lifestyle or going to live in a forest somewhere. No, it goes a lot deeper than that.

First, let's look at the nature of the universe. Well, Stoic philosophy tells us that everything exists in a balance and that there is a give and take state of things. This is what Zeno refers to when he speaks of the cycles of creation and destruction. By recognizing the validity of these cycles, their right to exist so to speak, we bring ourselves in greater line with reality.

Next, we have the nature of ourselves, or human beings. This is not about following one's true purpose like new age philosophy suggests. Remember the purpose of all human life is virtue. Instead, the method suggested here is to adopt the rational point of view that is inherent in all human beings.

Epictetus explains this point in one of his speeches where he suggests that a man is most animal-like when he gives into his emotions and his short-term urges. Using the example of a sheep, he points out that there is no difference between a man who satisfies his short-term urges, as guided by his emotions, and a sheep that goes about its day listening only to its stomach (Salzberger, 2019).

The difference is that the sheep is staying true to its nature but the man who does this isn't. Rationality is what separates man from a sheep, and human beings ought to use theirs at every juncture in order to attain virtue.

Attainment of Virtue

The previous point leads us right into this one, which is to say that the primary objective of all human beings as per Stoicism is the attainment of virtue. Virtue is the reward in and of itself. The feelings of satisfaction or joy you might receive are merely added bonuses.

Why does virtue play such an important role in our lives, and why is it a goal that ought to be prioritized? Well, virtue according to the Stoics is the behavior that is in the greatest accordance with nature. Why is it so important to act in accordance with nature? Because we are a part of it, and everything is connected.

Stoic thought presupposes the fact that virtue is the highest purpose of our lives, and this is why it is necessary to go back a little bit to the pre-Socratic era to understand from where this idea originated. Either way, the interconnectedness of things, as illustrated by how ancient philosophers pondered over the presence of the basic elements in the world existing within us in varying forms, was something that was already established.

Virtue is thus all about alignment. So, what are the tenets of virtue? Well, they are as follows:

- Self-discipline

- Fairness or a sense of justice

- Courage

- Wisdom

Self-discipline refers to one's ability to control his or her behavior and to act as rationally as possible at any given moment. The ability to act with humility and to avoid giving into short-term desires is a mark of self-discipline. A sense of justice recognizes the need to give back and to nurture the community since nothing exists in isolation.

Epictetus harps on this more than the others with his exhortations of duty to the commonwealth and to fellow man. By contrast, Zeno isn't too preoccupied with this. As for Seneca, he doesn't really care much for it and one can't blame him given his experiences in politics of the commonwealth.

Courage manifests in many forms, such as having the fortitude to see one's actions through and to also remain honest in the face of temptation. Courage is perhaps the most malleable principle when it comes to Seneca since he makes a big deal out of it but can be accused of hypocrisy in this regard. At best, one can say that his musings were depicting an ideal world and not the real hell that he was living in.

Lastly, we have wisdom, which is the exhortation to act with good judgment and other tenets of rationality. In short, all four elements of virtue deal with some aspect of rational behavior, and all of them address the outward nature of a man being influenced by control over his inner nature. I'm using man here to be in line with the language of the ancient philosophers. The word is meant to connote all human beings.

Stoicism mentions that the constant practice of all four elements is what constitutes virtue. Constant means exactly what you think: all the time. There is no slacking off when it comes to Stoicism! This should not be hard to do since the true reward is progress along the path of virtue, or at the very least, managing to stay on the path.

The ancient Stoics take great pains to point out that the material results of your effort are not the point of your actions. Whatever comes to you is out of your control. The only thing in your control is your virtue, so control the hell out of it (I might be paraphrasing that).

The Good, the Bad and the Indifferent

This is one of the most misunderstood and difficult to dissect tenets of Stoicism. It also happens to be one of the most powerful ones since it cuts right to the heart of many things through the power of logic. According to the Stoics, there are only three categories of things in this world: the good, the bad, and the indifferent.

The good things are those which are good for us, and these are the elements of virtue which we saw in the previous section. The bad ones are the exact opposite of those things. Then there's the indifferent category which encompasses everything else in between. This is where the confusion usually starts, so let's unpack this more.

Things such as health, wealth, and looks are all in the indifferent category. The idea is that these things are not necessary to live a virtuous life. Well, isn't some level of wealth desirable? Doesn't it make living a virtuous life easier by providing us with better options? Of course, it does. This is why the Stoics made a further categorization when it came to the indifferents: preferred and dispreferred.

Preferred indifferents are things like an abundance of good health and wealth, good looks, relationships and so on. These things certainly make life a lot easier and more joyful. However, the pursuit of these things must still be made within the boundaries of virtue. Pursuit of these outside of virtuous boundaries, that is within the bad boundary, will result in the attainment of dispreferred indifferents (which is just the opposite of the preferred ones).

So, what does all this mean? Well, first of all, it means that you can chase wealth and good looks and such. However, throughout the process your choices must be virtuous, and your chasing of these things must be carried out with the intention of increasing your virtue (Salzberger, 2019). If you're faced with a choice between a preferred indifferent and the good, it is the good that always takes precedence.

This means if you're faced with a choice of money or justice, you go with justice always. This is a perfectly brilliant framework with which to view life since it makes it possible for everyone to attain virtue. You can or cannot choose to go after the indifferents; it makes no difference in the big picture. At the end of the day, as Marcus wrote, everyone ends up in the same place, much like Alexander and his mule driver.

One of the consequences of this thought process is that it is far more preferable to endure poverty and sickness with dignity and as a consequence of virtuous action than to enjoy material wealth at the cost of a lack of virtue. This idea is a particularly powerful one and can be found in religions everywhere.

So, in the grand scheme of things, it is your behavior that determines everything. Lying to save a loved one from a sticky situation doesn't count as an act of honor since you compromised your virtue to do so. In this manner Stoicism manages to provide a behavioral guide for a lot of life's sticky situations in one fell swoop.

Doing Over Thinking

I touched upon this quality of Stoicism in the second chapter, but it pays to reiterate it here. Stoicism is all about doing. In this it stands in stark contrast to a lot of philosophy which is all about collecting and assimilating information. According to the Stoics, it isn't enough to just come up with great ideas; they're of no use unless they can be applied practically.

The path to virtue, as you've seen, is full of actions. You cannot exercise good judgment by just sitting around shoving chalupas into your mouth. You need to go out there and practice the tenets of Stoic philosophy for it to have any effect or benefit in your life. As Epictetus said, a lot of people end up getting shipwrecked when called into action (Salzberger, 2019).

The practice of cognitive behavioral therapy is founded on Stoic principles, and one of its main points is that in order to change your mind you need to take action. Changing habits and your self-image is an active process. It isn't enough to just read the information and then think about it. You have to actually put it into action and assimilate feedback in order to see the fruit of it.

When it comes down to it, ideas formed by action are far more valid than ideas born out of mere thought. So, get out there and apply these principles.

Equanimity

You're supposed to act in accordance with virtue, and if you do so you plod along the path of virtue and this is what brings good things into life, right? Well, not quite. Good or bad is beside the point. The very act of taking virtuous action is the reward. In other words, the work itself is the reward, not the result.

Why is this so? Well, consider the number of things that you control in a result. If you wish to make money in a business, for example, you can market your product to the best possible extent, you can set things up financially so that you earn a high profit margin, and you can hire the best employees who will design a great product. However, you do not control the mind of your consumer.

Ultimately, it is this person who is going to give you money. Therefore, to place the marker of success with something that is outside of yourself is a bit pointless. There's nothing you can do about it if it doesn't come through for you. Even if it does, what exactly did you control about its arrival? Not much. Therefore, the process is the reward.

But, if nothing is in your control, should you even care? Doesn't this mean that nothing matters very much? Well, no, because this is a very superficial reading of Stoicism. Remember that the only way to virtue is by taking action. So, doing nothing conflicts with this directly. Second, your reward is virtue, which is the highest possible thing anyone can aim for. So, claiming that nothing matters is false.

The real reason such thought occurs is because of the placing of too much value on the reward. This is a tough thing to let go of for a lot of people. In our modern world, we're taught to place goals and have all kinds of acronyms for them. Stoicism goes directly against this by saying that your goals are a preferred indifferent. Whether you reach them or not is not the point.

The point is the actions you take along the path. Can you see how liberating this is? How many times have you worried yourself sick with anxiety about reaching your goals or not reaching them on time? This kind of behavior is actually detrimental to your success. By placing so much importance on your goals, you end up strangling them.

Stoicism frees you from doing damage to yourself by helping you realize that your actions in the pursuit of virtue are what truly matter. Whether these come in pursuit of a goal or otherwise doesn't matter. All that matters is whether they are virtuous or not. End of story.

This ties in very nicely with the Buddhist idea of equanimity toward all things in life. Ultimately, a lot of things that happen to us don't matter very much at all. Stoicism helps us keep these things in proper view by reminding us of the fact that virtue and our actions are bigger than anything else we can dream of.

The practice of practicing misfortune is a direct result of this tenet. By forcing yourself to recognize that things might not go exactly as you want and that you'll still be ok, you're reinforcing this idea in your mind. Thus, you can see why the practice of Stoicism lies within the action itself.

Another Stoic technique is to establish the reserve clause. The reserve clause is best illustrated by Seneca, who said that he could sail across the ocean if nothing prevented him (Scott, 2018). The key here being that if nothing prevented him. Unexpected things happen all the time, so recognize that your goal and the universe need not agree on what the right path is.

When it comes down to it, your goals don't matter very much in the universal scheme of things. This is why the reserve clause is so powerful in helping us manage our expectations and in attaining our goals. Thus, we have what seems like a pessimistic outlook actually turn out to be the most liberating one of all.

Awareness

More than anything else, the practice of awareness is what separates the Stoic from the run of the mill person. The Stoics emphasized that practicing right action, with the purpose of attaining virtue, required a person to indulge in self-reflection and to be aware of their actions at all times.

This does not mean you need to shut off your feelings. Rather, it means you need to become aware or mindful of what's in your head and reflect on whether this is in line with your progress toward virtue or not. Is your reaction toward something that is within or outside your control? Asking yourself these questions in the moment is a key component of practicing Stoicism.

Awareness also wakes you up to the true nature of reality. The truth is that life is chaotic and we don't actually control a lot of things. There are just too many variables to consider. The Stoics used the analogy of a dog being tied behind a cart. The dog does not have any choice but to follow the cart wherever it goes. It has just two options: it can enjoy the ride voluntarily, or it can resist the cart's motion in a futile manner.

This seems like a defeatist attitude to life but if you examine it closely, you'll find that it is the most liberating one. With such an attitude you can be aware that both your mistakes and your achievements don't mean much in the overall scheme of things. You're still going to be dragged along by things out of your control.

All your achievements do is make the ride more pleasant, akin to the dog enjoying the scenery along the way. Hence, your preferred indifference and good actions make the view a whole lot better. Since you don't have a choice in the matter, you might as well accept this fact and do your best.

Journaling and reflection at the end of the day are methods of seeking improvement in your actions and figuring out the best way forward. The point is not to find fault with yourself but to simply look for places to improve. It is not about viewing your results but assessing whether your actions were in line with virtue.

Here again we see how Stoicism has a lot in common with the Buddhist practice of mindfulness or meditation. While Buddhism uses mediation as the ultimate practice via different techniques, Stoicism merely proposes it as one of many methods. Indeed, the ancient Stoics were not particularly aware of meditative practice but proposed one form of it via an end-of-day reflection anyway.

Chapter 5: Stoic Virtues

We've looked at the four Stoic pillars in the previous chapter when talking about how a person reaches the ultimate goal of virtue. To reiterate, these four pillars are prudence, courage, morality and moderation/discipline. It is worth it to dive deep into these concepts since they form the basis of the philosophy.

Leaders can take special lessons from the words of the Stoic philosophers on these subjects since they apply to all of life. While there are separate sections where the famous philosophers speak about leadership, all of that advice flows from understanding these four pillars.

Understand these and you'll cut to the heart of Stoicism pretty quickly.

Phronesis

The Stoics used this word to denote the first pillar of virtue. This Ancient Greek word loosely translates to prudence or practical wisdom. A quick note about translations. The only surviving Ancient Greek dictionary is one left behind by one of Plato's students. This is a bit problematic because a lot of the words used back then have different intentions behind them, even between philosophical schools.

The Platonists, or followers of Plato, used terms in a different manner compared to the Greek Stoics. Once the Ancient Greeks began fading from the scene and the Romans stepped in, a further layer of ambiguity was introduced thanks to Roman translation. A lot of the intent behind the words used by the Greeks is actually informed by the way the Romans translated them.

Who's to say how the Romans intended to use them though? Hence, when reading through these virtues, keep in mind that the modern English translations are loose fits. They don't exactly mean what was intended by the Stoics except for a few cases. Further complicating things is that English is a global language that extends far beyond native borders. Hence, there is a danger of things getting lost in translation. Therefore, explaining these concepts isn't as simple as simply listing out what they mean via translation.

Either way, we do have enough information to form a few conclusions. For one, the Platonists ideal to strive toward was termed sophia. Sophia refers to a high level, general wisdom which incorporates a lot of diverse subjects. Perhaps the best treatise on sophia is Aristotle's *Nicomachean Ethics* which dives into the study of good decision-making.

On the surface of it then, Aristotle was talking about prudence. He mentions in his works that for a person to make a good decision, he needs to have a thorough knowledge of his own first principles, but also needs to understand the epistemic principles (the root principles from which everything flows) of the subject at hand.

So, is this what the Stoics were on about when talking about prudence? Well, not quite. You see, the difference between sophia and phronesis lies in its applicability. Despite a single modern English word (prudence) covering both Ancient Greek words, the Ancient Greek meanings are different. The Stoic prudence refers to a more practical approach and involves the usage of discipline to make decisions (Robertson, 2018).

Sophia is more of a high-level wisdom, so it is important to not confuse the two concepts. Hence, the translation of phronesis to mean prudence instead of wisdom is more apt. So, what did the Stoics think of when talking about phronesis? Well, they simply referred to one's ability to discern between the good, bad and indifferent.

Using the principle of inversion, phronesis simply involves doing the exact opposite of qualities that would come under the umbrella of vice. Furthermore, phronesis involves a life lived in pursuit of truth and wisdom (sophia) (Pigliuci, 2016). From the main category of phronesis flows a number of other Stoic concepts dealing with things like rhetoric, conduct and logic.

Chrysippus, who was a famous student of Zeno's, counseled that the best form of rhetoric was a minimalist one where the objective was to help the listener understand the speaker's point. This has a lot of caveats to it, so he further clarifies by stating that the Stoic should communicate the truth in an honest and tactful manner. This is in stark contrast to not only the Cynical method of argument, which involved a good dose of insults (since nothing mattered) but was also contrary to Zeno's methods of rhetoric (Pigliuci, 2016).

Above all else, the Stoics contended that a wise man's highest quality is his ability to offer good counsel to himself, not just others. Of all the Stoics, Chryssipus is the one who is the most looked up to when it comes to understanding the field of logic from a Stoic perspective. After all, prudence is all about offering good counsel, so it follows that some study of logic is necessary. There is the danger of getting twisted with jargon when it comes to logic, so I'm going to keep this as high level as possible, with all due apologies to the computer programmers amongst you.

Logic by itself is a fascinating field of study when it comes to the Ancient Greeks. They were obsessed with developing better decision-making methods and constantly debated it. Thus, the debate of what constitutes good logic is a subject by itself and is not a subset of phronesis. The field of logic included principles from subjects such as physics, epistemology and ethics.

Keep in mind that the physics of that era was very different from what we think of physics these days. Physics back then denoted the force between things and their relation to one another, so there was a fair bit of naturology and God forces involved. This often seems incongruent to modern readers, but this is because of there not being a good enough translation in modern English to signify what the ancients were on about.

Chrysippus is credited with developing the first propositional logic which is actually very similar to the logic found in computer science textbooks today. Boolean logic is thought to be an almost like-for-like copy of what Chrysippus had in mind. I say "almost" and "very similar" because none of Chrysippus' work has survived to the modern day.

Stoic logic is based on five rules for inference. The first rule is that of propositions. A proposition is a statement of fact and the first step is to consider simple propositions. For example, "Dion is walking" (this comes directly from a work which quotes Chrysippus) (Scott, 2018).

From this simple statement, we can build more complex propositions using connectives (modern logical language). The Stoics used the conditional (if x, then y), paraconditional (since x, then y), conjunction (both x and y), disjunction (either x or y), causal (because x, y), the more (more x than y) and the less (less x than y).

Once the complex propositions are developed, the next step was to apply indemonstrables to them. These were the standard indemonstrables which were borrowed from Plato's syllogisms and were modus ponens, modus tollens, negated conjunctions, exclusive disjunction with positive, and exclusive disjunction with negative (Scott, 2018).

You'll notice I've been getting extremely academic here. Well, don't worry because there isn't any more to come. What Chrysippus thought of the remaining three steps is not known, nor do any of the later philosophers talk in-depth about any of this. Given the importance of practicality, the Stoics were more concerned with applying the rules rather than explaining them over and over again.

The overall lesson of phronesis remains a simple one despite all this. In all decisions, considering what can and cannot be controlled and acting on that which can be controlled is what determines prudence. Remember that prudence is different from wisdom even if modern English doesn't quite make the difference explicit.

Dikaiosune

This word pertains to the Stoic pillar of justice. At this point, again we run into translation issues since modern meaning and the Stoic meaning are two different things. The Stoics referred to justice as an all-encompassing path to virtue, and this included both one's actions toward oneself as well as the effects of one's actions on larger society (Robertson, 2018).

In other words, wisdom applied in the pursuit of justice had dual aims. The first was to ensure the individual walked along the path of virtue. The second dealt with the effects of an individual's actions on society as a whole. In modern parlance we can call this social justice. Now, this is a trigger word for many people with a bunch of political meanings flowing from it.

So, let's dive into this concept a bit deeper and unpack what it is *not*. Social justice is a commendable pursuit and is frankly a natural one. However, the dimensions it has taken on these days, including the perverted meanings associated with "safe spaces," "trigger warnings" and so on have nothing to do with Stoicism.

This doesn't mean that Stoic social justice is a cold-blooded beast. It's just that modern society has gone off the rails in pursuit of political correctness. This is especially true in America, where all matters of social justice involve political rhetoric and, in the end, nothing gets done beyond a few tweets being fired off in an outrage cycle playing itself out on social media.

Safe to say, this is not what the Stoics had in mind. Stoicism doesn't explicitly mention this, but in a lot of its tenets the philosophy does reflect the wisdom of the middle path that Buddhist philosophy is centered around. This is truer of Zeno than it is of the later Stoics, but the thought process holds throughout (Robertson, 2018).

Social justice and notions of equality were a natural outcome of Stoicism since, as we learned previously, the Stoics viewed everyone as belonging to one collective soul that emanated from universal consciousness. Hence, it made perfect sense to help out a fellow human being in distress.

However, there is a contradiction that can arise. The outcome of social justice when directed beyond oneself is something an individual cannot control. So, how does this reconcile with the goal of social justice also requiring benefitting the world? Well, this is where the concept of the reserve clause comes into the picture. The reserve clause is simple yet powerful: A Stoic will do his best to help his fellow man, fate permitting.

This concept of the reserve clause acknowledges that things out of our control may or will affect the desired outcomes. Hence, the Stoic goal of justice is an internal one and is concerned with action and intention that is being expressed. Cicero used the analogy of an archer who fires at a target only to see his target moved at the last instant to describe this thought process (Robertson, 2018).

The action of pulling the bow and intending to hit what was in front of him is what counts toward the path of virtue. The actual result will vary but it is preferred that it is favorable. According to Marcus Aurelius, justice contains two qualities: kindness and fairness.

Kindness is simply the absence of cruelty. Applying the traditional Stoic method of good and bad not existing, there is no difference between kindness directed at a friend or an enemy. It is fully possible to be kind to an enemy by not wishing revenge upon them or trying to educate them as to the folly of their ways, assuming proper wisdom has determined that your way is correct.

This discerning of whether our actions are right or wrong is what fairness is all about, and it involves meditation (that is thought) on our own actions. The exact method of doing this is not prescribed since the later Stoics seem to have taken

Chrysippus' methods of logical deduction to heart and have treated them as obvious.

Either way, a lot of this is common sense and this is why the Stoics placed a good deal of weight on the intention behind the action and evaluation of the outcome for clues as to where one could improve. After all, this is what the end of day journaling is all about.

Thus, the Stoic dedicates himself to the common good and welfare of his fellow man and is supremely concerned with the wisdom of his own actions. Fate permitting, his actions will result in the common good being realized, but since he has no control over this, all he can do is focus on his intention and the development of his wisdom.

Sophrosune

This pillar refers to the practice of temperance in the pursuit of virtue. More than any other principle, it is here that a lot of people trip themselves up. You see, Stoicism is an all or nothing philosophy. When it comes to self-discipline, this happens to be a particular problem for a lot of people.

A lot of us tend to be disciplined in one area of our lives and then let go in other areas, seeking a release from the discipline. According to the Stoics, the path of self-discipline is the same as freedom itself. This principle again echoes the thoughts of Buddhist philosophy and even finds its way down to contemporary religious practices (Robertson, 2018).

So, what does temperance really mean? Well, one alternative translation of this is the spirit of moderation. In other words, avoid the extremes of anything. Now, hopefully you understand why I've been harping on and on about the need to avoid adopting fundamentalist beliefs about anything, including Stoicism.

Anyway, back to our topic. So, moderation in everything is great, but how does one recognize it? Well, this is where the Stoics applied the principle of inversion and illustrated their point by mentioning that the absence of vice and its damaging effects are indicators of the presence of moderation.

Note that a lot of indicators of vice, such as ill-health and so on, are ultimately a part of the dispreferred indifferents category. So, does this mean that the attainment of a preferred indifferent, such as wealth, is an indicator of virtue? Well, not quite. This is why the indifferents category exists, after all. The pursuit of a preferred indifferent is well and good, but the underlying intention should be the attainment of virtue.

As long as the actions taken to attain the indifferent are in line with that of moderation, then an individual is living the Stoic way. Note that extreme attachment to a preferred indifferent is to ignore the pillar of temperance. Using this line of thought, a lot of modern ideas, such as the law of attraction, have their fundamental problems solved.

In modern pop philosophical parlance, the act of temperance is simply the act of letting go of the need to achieve your goal. You may want it but recognize that you don't need it in order to be happy. The Stoics used virtue to highlight this point by placing goals in the indifferents category and virtue above all else. Quite an elegant solution to a problem that has troubled human beings throughout the ages.

The enforcement of discipline also becomes far easier when adopting a Stoic viewpoint since pleasure is an indifferent. Therefore, foregoing it is not a big deal and a Stoic is far more willing to sacrifice it in the pursuit of his ultimate goal. If anything, not giving his pleasure primary importance is, by itself, a virtuous act according to Stoicism.

Hence, the application of self-discipline doesn't involve any sacrifice. If anything, it is the addition of a benefit to one's life. Hence, self-discipline equals freedom, which is the same as the path toward virtue.

Andreia

This is the simplest one of all the pillars to decipher since there is no possibility of mistranslation. Perhaps this speaks to the human condition but that is neither here nor there. Andreia refers to courage or the ability to face one's fears. This is a paradoxical quality because, as Seneca observes, courage requires the presence of fear for it to mean anything (Robertson, 2018).

Stoics' views on courage are pretty similar to the Sophist view. Much like how Socrates denoted the difference between recklessness and true courage as being wisdom, so do the Stoics. A theoretical strain that you can undertake within this pillar is the concept of proto-passions. Proto-passions explain why the presence of fear does not mean the absence of virtue.

Epictetus illustrates this point using the story of a Stoic teacher who was trapped on a sinking ship while on his way to Rome. This is actually a true story, but the identity of the teacher in question is not known. Some scholars speculate that the person in this story is actually Marcus Aurelius' teacher. Either way, the ship is sinking in a terrific gale and it is clear that help might not arrive in time.

The Stoic teacher is scared out of his mind and is gripping the sides of the boat in complete fear, as the boat sinks further. Unlike the other sailors though, the Stoic is not screaming out for help or praying in terror to God for mercy. This highlights the Stoic quality of courage as described by this pillar of Stoic virtue.

Proto-passions are simply natural animal-like instincts that pop into our heads when confronted with fear. Human beings are a part of nature and are subject to the same natural processes as animals are. The difference lies in the application of rationality. Perhaps the best way to describe this is to paraphrase Victor Frankl, who mentioned that there is a gap between the stimulus and the reaction (Robertson, 2018).

It is in that gap that wisdom lies. The Stoic teacher knows he's very likely to drown (spoiler alert: he doesn't) and is fearful of this. This is the proto-passion flaring up which reflects his natural animal instinct of survival. How he reacts to this stimulus is what makes him a Stoic.

The absence of fear is also not a sign of courage. This is simply being reckless. To have no fear in a truly threatening situation is to deny the existence of proto-passions. In other words, to say that one doesn't experience fear is a lie which is a vice.

Admittedly, some of this might seem obvious but again, you must read all of this while keeping in mind the age in which it was written. This was a time when men were expected to die as a matter of routine when defending their walls since defeat meant genocide at best. Fear and courage were hotly debated topics within some cultures, such as the Spartans, going to extreme lengths to beat it out of their men.

All of this led to fear being painted as a primarily feminine trait, and for a major branch of philosophy to come out and say that courage required fear to be valid was a bold move. Even if soldiers knew the truth of this statement, they were hardly expected to admit it.

The announcement of this Stoic virtue is thus a Stoic act in itself. The pursuit of the common good and truth was above everything else for the Stoics and was the path to virtue. In doing so, they fulfilled the requirements of both this pillar as well as phronesis. All three of Seneca, Epictetus, and Marcus talk of the quality of courage and the necessity of fear being present in their works.

This brings to a close our look at the four pillars of Stoicism. Admittedly, a single chapter is not good enough, and even an entire book might be too brief. For further reading on these topics, the writings of Donald Robertson are particularly illuminating.

Chapter 6: Modern Stoicism

In the late 20th century, Stoicism saw a huge rise in popularity. One of the reasons for this has already been laid out in a previous chapter, dealing with the increasing uncertainty in our world, while not containing high levels of negative instability. Whatever you think of the rise of Stoicism, there's no denying that these ancient principles find themselves relevant to this day.

So, is there a difference between ancient and modern Stoic thought? Aside from deeply theoretical discourses, in a word: no. So, why dedicate a chapter to this? Well, it is worth taking the time to examine how Stoicism can be applied in our world today.

You see, things such as virtue and the pursuit of wisdom are not deemed worthy of our time these days. Of course, all of us see the wisdom of these things, but our thinking has been warped by the scientific process which has existed for so many years now. The scientific process requires proof above all else and is rigidly based on rational thought.

Philosophy doesn't lend itself very well to the scientific process. Evidence of this is the fact that the most popular and respected modern philosophers are those who are best at adopting a scientific process when discussing philosophy. All of this results in deeply theoretical discussions which are not readily accessible, even if they are available to peruse.

This is in stark contrast to ancient times when philosophy was viewed as being the duty of every single person to adopt and live. I mean, the name Stoicism itself is derived from the public place from which Zeno began shouting at everyone.

This sort of thing doesn't happen today. The corners of Hyde Park and Union Square (modern day stoas, if you will) are filled with religious fundamentalists shouting at us that the world is coming to an end. It is a sad state of affairs indeed.

Interaction in the modern world has changed since ancient times, and a large part of this has to do with the internet. As an example, consider the fact that outrage has actually become a tactic to garner attention and is a required attribute for many popular media outlets to have any hope of success.

So, let's take a step back and see why Stoicism has popular appeal in today's world and how you can apply it to specific thought processes that all of us deal with on a daily basis.

The Spread of Stoicism

I'd like to point out that what follows in this section is my opinion and that you ought to apply a healthy dose of critical thought to whatever is being said. In short, don't take my word for it. Find your own truth if it really matters to you.

The reasons for the viral spread of Stoicism come down to three things:

1. Increasing uncertainty

2. Ease of information exchange

3. Relevance

Increasing Uncertainty

Before the boom of social media there were institutions we could rely on to supply us with facts. Sure, some of these were unbelievably biased, but at least we knew this going in. It was easy to make a judgment call on whether or not the information being given to us was biased in any way.

Fast forward to today and you have news stations and reporters quoting tweets as sources. Social media is driven by engagement. In other words, Facebook wants you to keep coming back to it, and the only way it can do this is to get you to associate positive feelings with it. It does this by giving you exactly what you want.

Even Google, the so-called organizer of information, shows recommended stories which align closely with your own interests. This is harmless when it comes to things such as sports where it makes sense for you to follow your team's progress. However, when it comes to hot button issues like politics and social problems, this is the worst thing to do.

Consider that the most maligned social network/modern social company is currently YouTube. Is this because the platform delivers poor quality content? Not really. It's mostly because the stuff it shows you is irrelevant, and its recommended choices are completely useless. We've come to demand engagement from our social media, but we don't know where to draw the line.

As a result, apathy is at an all-time high and critical thought is not prioritized in mass media anymore. Sure, mass media is not innocent in any of this, but the point is that everything has been dumbed down to being mere entertainment. The ridiculous election of 2016 proves how dumb mainstream dialogue is.

The irony is that the more engaged we're becoming with our social media channels, the less relevance they have to our real lives. Does our life improve a lot depending on how many social media likes one receives? If you have a business, sure.

How about a personal profile though? A like on a great photograph doesn't change the reality that you live in a dumpster.

People are slowly finding out that the social currency these likes and retweets generate has no relevance to real life. So, where is one to turn? Mass media houses are simply not trusted anymore and are simply one extreme these days. Compound this with the fact that the world is changing faster than ever before. Compare the pop culture moments of the previous decade to this one.

Off the top of my head, I can safely count at least double the number of "things" that became pop culture moments. Remember when "Gangnam Style" was the bomb? Yeah, that was in 2012. Poor old Psy didn't even receive fifteen minutes. He burned bright and then faded away from mainstream relevance.

Contrast this with William Hung from the previous decade, who couldn't even sing and stayed relevant for far longer. My point is, the ground is shifting beneath our feet. Large numbers of people in our society feel left behind and have no idea what to do. All in all, it's not too different from what was going on in Ancient Rome around Seneca's time.

Ease of Information Exchange

At this point in time, it's easier than ever to go viral. After all, everything is connected. Google knows what you're doing on YouTube, Facebook will record your phone conversations and use it serve you better ads if you allow it, and the governments of the world simply steal all the data they can lay their hands on (I'm joking of course...or not).

It's not difficult for information created in one corner of the globe to find its way to the other end of the world within a few minutes. This has helped Stoicism gain greater popularity and, ironically, the negative effects of interconnectedness have also helped the philosophy experience a resurgence.

There is more information but there is far more noise. Every oaf with a blog has an opinion that can be easily disseminated, and outlets such as Facebook Live or YT Live have made launching a media channel easier than ever before. What results is a steady stream of outrage cycles.

Remember the time when Colin Kaepernick kneeling was a referendum on American democracy? And how the NFL's response to Trump piggybacking on the issue was comically inept? How they went from "kneel" to "please don't kneel" to "don't you dare kneel" to "kneel in the tunnel" and finally to "we'll fund some no name program, so please stop"?

Yeah, me neither. The Steelers just got blown away by Brady/Belichick again and somehow the Pats are going to go to the Super Bowl. Again.

So, what is noise and what is real? We only have so much time on our hands, so what should we focus on? Questions like these have become extremely important since more than ever, we're realizing that we are literally architects of our reality. What we see on the internet is a reflection of what we're paying attention to more than ever before.

The problem isn't in creating what we want. The problem is figuring out what we ought to create.

Relevance

This is where the universality of Stoicism comes into play. There's no hand wringing and no need to figure out deep philosophical theories. Stoicism fits both the modern philosophy bro as well as the deeper thinker who likes some meat to chew on. On a shallow level, the principles of Stoicism pass the skim test.

People don't read anymore, they skim. Think back to how you react when you come across new content. There's so much stuff out there you need to figure out if this new piece of information is worth your time. So, you skim.

After this point, the philosophy bro checks out of the process because he has to go brag about how Stoicism is lit and why he's a Stoic because he's getting back to nature by munching on his locally sourced avocado toast layered with Guatemalan bee poop and chia seed essence. Because nature.

Either way Stoicism gets a like. The deeper thinker who goes back and takes the time to read through the philosophy finds enough material to ruminate on and hence, even that demographic is covered.

All in all, Stoicism simply fits well with the current state of things. Will it always be this way? Probably not. There will come a time when it will go out of fashion. That is irrelevant to you though. What matters is what you can do to make your life just a bit easier and drown out the incessant noise.

Basic Tenets for Modern Life

Having finished that rant, it's now time for me to come back to philosopher mode. Don't worry, I'm not going to bore you with a deep discussion of the ethics of layering bee poop on your toast. Instead, what I will do is highlight a few simple practices which are particularly relevant to modern life and which will enable you to handle it better.

Pondering the Externals

In the words of Epictetus, what is it that we spend most of our attention on? Who do we admire the most? Why should we be surprised that fear and distress are the norm with us (Salzberger, 2019)? The externals are what the Stoics named everything that exists outside of ourselves. This is a very rigid definition. So, basically anything that exists outside of your own mind is an external.

The entire point of observing equanimity and realizing that there are a large number of things you don't control is to help you cope with the effect of externals on your life. Things like politics, weather, your career situation, and so on are all things which have aspects within them that you cannot control.

Admittedly, some of them can be controlled more than the others, but the underlying truth is that you can only control your actions. So, instead of focusing on the external aspects you cannot control, focus on what you can. You cannot control the constant bombardment of negativity you receive when you consume media. You can control your choice to consume it though. Hence, exercise it.

The Stoic mindset is a solution-oriented one since it relentlessly focuses on what you can do, not what you feel. Even analysis of the current situation, which might be good or bad, is carried out with a view to do something about it. Hence, by forcing you to take action, Stoicism removes you from inside your head and gets you going.

When you begin to focus on your actions, you'll realize the level of noise you are subjecting yourself to. This way, the times you do choose to relax and consume social media, you'll end up being hyper aware of what type of information you're receiving since you will not be inured to having your senses dulled all the time.

Pondering Death

Well, this got serious in a hurry, didn't it? Like a lot of Stoic thought, this one looks morbid on the outside but is actually a liberating philosophy. The Stoics believed that old age is no guarantee of a life well lived. What they meant by that was that there is a difference between existing and living.

A life lived in pursuit of virtue is a very different existence from one where a person merely reacts to what is happening around them. This is precisely what is going on in our world right now. Our attention is being pulled in every direction, and by paying heed to all this noise, none of us have any time to live.

To live is to understand what your life is all about and what are the good, bad, and indifferent aspects of it. How are you structuring your days? Are they in pursuit of the path of virtue, or are you giving way too much importance to the dispreferred indifferents? The stuff you see on social media, with people dying to post their latest vacation snaps in exchange for a few likes, is this a preferred or dispreferred indifferent?

At the very least we can agree with the fact that none of them are desirable things that lead to virtue. The world is far too focused these days on indifferents, and the true goals of everything get twisted into something else. Social media itself was meant to bring everyone together. Instead, we've turned it into a tool to push ourselves further apart.

Bring perspective back to your life by pondering how well you can live it. What are the really important things to you? By figuring this out, you will also figure out how to die well. As Seneca advises, be aware of death in everything you do. You cannot control death since this is an external. With this in mind, how would you live your life?

Start from there and move forward.

Presence

Presence can be thought of being a combination of two qualities: focus and a practical state of mind. A practical state of mind is one that is rational and recognizes the importance of the path. As an aside, there is a divergence between the definition of presence in Stoicism and Buddhism, with the latter including emotions within its model.

Either way, the goal of achieving presence is something that has also increased of late in the public eye. Meditation has been packaged and converted into something called mindfulness, which is a bit like offering someone a banana and giving them just the skin. Ancient Eastern spirituality has been conveniently packaged and now comes in shiny little Buddha statues.

Consuming all these things is not the way to develop presence. The only way to be present is to be present. You have to actively practice it. It isn't more complicated than that. This is not to say that it is simple. Stoicism doesn't bother with packaging of any kind since it doesn't lend itself to it very well, no matter how many new age entrepreneurs try to do so.

The practice of equanimity is tied to being present. By letting things occur and by simply letting them pass through you, you're allowing life to happen. You'll remain focused on what you can control; that is yourself. Therefore, to remain equanimous and to allow things to happen is the most active state of being, despite sounding passive.

Life happens, so give yourself a reserve clause. Acknowledge the randomness in life and watch as it blossoms. Of course, don't do it for this reason. Remember, the results of your life are the indifferents. Virtue is what matters above all else.

Chapter 7: Stoic Principles for a Modern Leader

Leaders have always existed in many forms. The President of the country is as much a leader as the person who is running a small business employing three people. Both situations have roughly the same broad demands, even if the details vary widely.

Stoic thought on leadership is confined almost exclusively to Marcus Aurelius for understandable reasons. While Seneca has also produced treatises, most notably *On Guilt*, his words are tarnished by the fact that he produced these right on cue when threatened with an executioner. So, who knows where Seneca's focus was?

The interesting thing about studying Marcus is that almost all of his thoughts are essentially Epictetus' principles applied for the role the former held in his life. This is not a criticism of Marcus, merely an observation. In what can be construed as criticism, I will say that Marcus is often thought of as being the last great Western Roman emperor, but this is a slightly false narrative.

During his time, there isn't any reliable evidence of Marcus being considered a great emperor or being anything beyond a middling one. His singular claim to fame is his *Meditations*, so he was probably a better Stoic than he was an emperor. This being said, it's not as if the man was incompetent.

The point I'm making is to make sure you evaluate Marcus' sayings in the right context. This was not an emperor on par with Julius Caesar or Augustus ("Marcus Aurelius," 2019).

His reign stands out because of the sheer incompetence of the rulers that followed him that led to the eventual demise of Rome as a world-conquering power.

So, keep this perspective in mind when reading anything to do with Stoicism and leadership.

Leading as a Job

Musing on the nature of leadership, Marcus writes that there are three sorts of people. The first carry out a favor and immediately expect one in return and demand it. The second carry it out and don't demand it but make a note in their mental ledger that something is owed. The last give without expectation of anything in return. Marcus likens this third type of person to a vine that gives grapes year after year without demanding anything in return (Holiday, 2018).

His point is that a leader ought to be the third type. The leader is a far more mature person than the general populace because he recognizes the need for someone to step up and provide service to the people. The leader does this not because of some goodness of his heart, although that helps, but rather due to the fact that it happens to be his job. It is just what he does, much like how fish swim without thinking.

Carrying out a task for the sake of it and not for the recognition is the true hallmark of a great leader according to Marcus.

On Ambition

The nature of leadership in most situations calls for the leader to have a lot of ambition. It is a curious trait amongst humans in that we seek leadership from those who are the most self-absorbed. As a result, the true leaders are revealed only when they're thrust into a role they never expected to be in and find that they wear it well.

Marcus, like other Stoics, cautioned against the dangers of overriding ambition which compromised the wellbeing of the collective in favor of a single person. The goal of leadership was not glory but to ensure the wellbeing of the people underneath the ruler. This is a fascinating point because it serves as an insight into a number of Marcus' actions during his time as a ruler (Holiday, 2018).

When really dissected, this notion seems to suggest that it is better to be a middling ruler as per the history books than an Alexander. While the latter was a conqueror and has been remembered for ages, how many rulers do we remember who put the happiness of their subjects ahead of their ambition? Not very many.

This, in a nutshell, is the irony of leadership. A truly great leader is one who will probably not be recognized as such by his subjects thanks to the lack of the traditional markers of great leadership. Ambition enacted in line with virtue is a justifiable indifferent. When one acts on ambition to the detriment of virtue, a leader isn't a true leader anymore.

Ego and self-glorification receive the same treatment as ambition. Marcus takes great pains to remind himself of how small and mortal he is. This isn't mere lip service; the aim of these statements is to remind himself that his highest goal is still virtue, and that he needs to take care that he doesn't corrupt his mind with his own ego.

Calmness

This is a lesson that Marcus learned while under the tutelage of Antonius Pius, his predecessor to the throne. Marcus was privileged in that he got to observe not just one but two emperors during his lifetime. The first example was provided by Hadrian. Marcus observed that Hadrian had a short temper and that an environment of tension prevailed over any scene over which he presided.

In contrast, Pius was the opposite and engendered a feeling of calm amongst his subjects. In the long run, Marcus reflected, it was better for a leader to remain calm, no matter what came at him, as opposed to allowing himself to be flustered. His advice is quite practical in this regard.

By preparing himself and anticipating the fact that things will likely go wrong, the leader can remain calm no matter how bad the situation gets. This negative expectation approach might not sit well with some of those reading this, but it seems to have worked well for Marcus.

When reading his words on this subject, we must keep in mind that Marcus often described himself as someone who suffered from a ferocious temper (Holiday, 2018). So, is the exhortation to calm meant to be a reminder to himself to not lose his cool, or is its emphasis intended as a warning to everyone? We'll never know the truth of this.

Either way, the wisdom behind the need for staying calm is undeniable, and every leader should strive to be the one who remains firm when things are falling apart around them. In doing so, he earns the respect of those who follow him as well as manages to divert his own attention to figuring out the solutions to the problems presenting themselves.

What more could one ask for in a leader? Interestingly, this is a motto that the Navy SEALS live by. "Calm is contagious" is one of their more famous maxims.

Expect to Be Wrong

The leader's primary concern is with truth. This is not meant to be some deep philosophical statement. Rather, Marcus' point in making this statement is that the leader should always strive to unearth the root causes of situations. This requires him to keep an open mind and to incorporate feedback.

Again, here were see Marcus' qualities of an ideal leader go squarely up against what we usually see from most people in leadership positions. It is the norm to simply accept what people in power say and move on, rather than risk antagonizing them. If this is true now, one can imagine how true it must have been back then.

So, for the most powerful man in the world to say that he expects to be wrong and that he expects his advisers to point out his mistakes is quite a remarkable statement. Of course, the logic behind this saying is not suspect. However, the question of how exactly a leader is supposed to instill this environment in his subjects does arise.

Marcus isn't very clear on this and can't be expected to be so since the *Meditations* are his own record of personal reflection and weren't written to be a manual for leadership. Still, it is useful to examine records of Marcus' own life to find clues as to how exactly he went about doing this.

The answer seems to lie in the practice of Stoicism itself, especially in the exercise of calm. Perhaps this is really why

Marcus places such a huge importance on the quality of calmness after all. The Stoic philosophy enabled Marcus to constantly reinforce his own mortality and enforced humility within himself.

Thus, it is not hard to see how he must have created an environment of open feedback around himself. While it is unrealistic to presume that it was like this all the time, the very fact that Marcus makes an effort is significant. After all, there aren't many leaders who do this these days, so for him to practice this all the way back then took some effort.

Maintain Control Over Passions

The word passions as used in Ancient Rome was very different from the context we use it in these days. Passion merely meant acting out in an irrational manner and in opposition to what was the best manner of attending to things. This point is an extension of the previous point on remaining calm.

The leader should always strive to control his anger and remind himself that it isn't "manly" to become enraged (Holiday, 2018). If anything, civility and gentleness are more human qualities, and this is where true strength lies. A person who gives in to anger and discontent loses his strength to rule and to influence.

More than anything else, by losing control over himself, he is placing far too much importance over the externals and is trying to control things which cannot be controlled. Such a leader then is doomed to fail, not to mention disrespected amongst the ranks of his people.

Calmness in the face of provocation is far more intimidating than anger. This doesn't mean to say that the leader ought to accept every insult with a smile. The point is that he should always seek to maintain calm in all situations. In doing so, he will deliver a far stronger message to his enemies than any amount of anger ever could.

This principle is almost always understood by elite-level athletes. The concept of trash talk exists solely to cause an imbalance within the opponent. The ones who remain calm are almost never trash-talked since there's no point in trying to affect them. A good example of this was Joe Louis, the boxing champ.

All in all, according to Marcus, the nearer a man is to a calm mind, the closer he is to his ultimate source of strength.

The Collective Above the Individual

This particular point is liable to send the Ayn Rand crowd flying into a rage, but Marcus was all about placing the collective benefit of the world above himself. Rather remarkably, he described himself as being a citizen of the world rather than just of Rome. Marcus' actions don't quite bear out his words in this regard, but he can be excused if his enemies didn't quite believe in this same philosophy.

Stoicism believes in the interconnectedness of everything and of everything emanating from a collective consciousness. To serve the collective is to ultimately live in line with this consciousness. As such, this idea was far ahead of its time and it is only now that we see our world and societies waking up to this fact. Even now, in fact, there is massive resistance to this idea and how it needs to be implemented. Witness the refugee crisis and the manner in which solutions have been implemented and the criticism such policies have engendered.

So, for an Ancient Roman emperor to proclaim that the whole world was one and the same and that everyone was equal was a pretty remarkable act. Marcus describes his notion saying that what isn't good for the hive isn't good for the bee (Holiday, 2018). He even emphasizes the inverse of this argument in a separate portion of his book by saying that the thing that doesn't harm the community cannot harm the individual.

In today's highly individualistic age, this might not be widely accepted as a political treatise. However, the emphasis here is on the right way to live. To live correctly is to acknowledge that everything and everyone depends on one another, and that to wish harm on someone else is to merely wish harm upon yourself.

You might be wondering that saying all of this is one thing but implementing it is another. How well did Marcus do with regard to this tenet of his? Not very well, to be honest. As mentioned earlier, his reign was one of constant battles. In some he was provoked, and in others he was the aggressor. In some he had zero control, while in some he had full control over the policies which determined outcomes.

A common complaint against Marcus is his persecution of Christians in the traditionally barbaric Ancient Roman way. Given that the man has no opportunity to explain himself, perhaps we can note that this was common practice at the time and that he didn't increase such persecution but merely continued it.

Second, Marcus was a human being above all else. Remember that his *Meditations* are reminders to himself to correct his actions or to enforce correct behavior in anticipation of the coming day. Reading it as a political treatise is to read it wrong. The spirit of it is what matters above all else.

Acknowledge Responsibility

The leader is the one in charge of the organization, and it is with him that ultimate responsibility lies. He doesn't have anyone else to blame or turn to when things go wrong. Some might say this is a huge burden, and Marcus agreed with this notion. As a method of preventing his mind from being compromised off its path, he reminded himself to accept and acknowledge the responsibility that was placed on him.

This is an extremely powerful act of control and is a liberating one. If a leader only judges his own actions as being good or bad and believes that it is his actions that he can control that ultimately lead to success or failure, there is no justification or even room to blame someone else for misfortune.

Thus, by taking responsibility, the leader puts himself in a place of being able to make a reasoned choice, which is the ultimate aim for leadership.

Realize Your Power of Consent

A common complaint that leaders have is that it is extremely difficult to remain calm and equanimous because of the fact that they do not control a vast number of things. Simply put, they aren't responsible for the output of those beneath them. This attitude highlights a number of mistakes according to Marcus.

First is the fact that focusing on the results of the process is the wrong thing to do. This is not so much what Marcus says as it is a general Stoic belief. Second is the assumption that a leader can do better if only he just controlled more things. How can a person ever know how things will turn out? No matter what he does, there are far too many variables in the equation.

Lastly, and this is the point Marcus explicitly makes, annoyance and a disturbed mind is not caused by the actions of those around us (Holiday, 2018). Instead, it is caused by our assent to giving those stimuli permission to disturb us. In other words, it's not the constantly barking dog that is annoying. It is your act of allowing yourself to be annoyed that annoys you.

The Stoics refer to this action of allowing annoyance or anything into the mind as hypolepsis. This literally means "taking up" and refers to how people take up burdens into their minds and blame those around them. Instead, it is they themselves who are at fault and it is their action that is the cause, not the conditions around them.

Hence, the wise leader realizes that other people are not the cause but merely the target of their anger. The cause lies well within them and this means it can be controlled. Control your own perceptions and you'll control the world around you. Give things consent to annoy you and they promptly will.

Remain Grounded

Marcus' *Meditations* is full of exhortations to himself reminding himself to not get carried away by his title and his rank. This was the wealthiest and most powerful man in his world. He constantly reminds himself that the ultimate goal of life is virtue and that the path one takes toward it determines the quality of the life one has lived, not the indifferents he amassed during his life.

Leaders often find that success changes things around them and that it can be difficult to handle the fallout from it. This is because of the fact that while success is great, a focus on the end result of achieving success is likely to result in it going to one's head. A leader who delivers success against great odds is likely to be placed on a pedestal by his subordinates and as a result remove himself further from reality.

This is why it is crucial for leaders to remind themselves of their mortality and to remain grounded at all times. By reminding themselves that it is not success but virtue that is the ultimate goal, a leader can remain oriented along the right path. Not doing this will likely result in ambition and pride corrupting the goals of the collective and failure automatically results.

Above all else, a leader must let his reason shine through and not his whims. Successful leaders often develop a sixth sense which is nothing more than their egos trying to assert themselves in various ways. By reminding himself to let his reason shine through and by keeping himself grounded, the leader can ensure that he doesn't undo the good work he has achieved.

Plan Ahead

Marcus spoke about the importance of planning by reminding himself that he was to take no random actions and that every action of his must be grounded in underlying principles. This is the Ancient Roman way of saying "failing to plan is planning to fail."

There are a lot of variables in life and things happen that we have no control over. This is perfectly fine. However, preparation never stops. The chaos that will ensue due to a leader not preparing well and planning ahead will place him in a bad position when the unexpected happens.

In such a position, the leader will then have to fight the twin negatives of dealing with the unexpected as well as coping with the disappointment that things are not going his way. This places him in too deep a hole, and it is unlikely that success can be achieved from such a position.

Whatever you think of Marcus, there is no denying that his exhortations to himself make a lot of sense for leaders everywhere. While he doesn't offer any new insight in terms of Stoic theory, he certainly does a great job of illustrating how the application of Stoicism enabled him to remain sane when things were crumbling apart.

An examination of the reign of his successor, Commodus, is proof of how bad things could have gone for Rome and how Marcus could have lost his mind under the pressure he dealt with. Great emperor or not, Marcus remains a shining example of the wisdom inherent in Stoicism and its applicability to leadership at all levels.

Chapter 8: Stoic Misconceptions — Myths Debunked

Stoicism has a number of myths attached to it. This isn't surprising because Stoic philosophy goes against a lot of modern notions about positivity and attracting things into your life. I'm not saying that those philosophies are wrong, by the way. Just that the prevalent philosophical environment biases us to think about the Stoics as being pessimists.

The truth is that Stoic philosophy is all about liberating oneself through discipline. I've explained how this works in a previous chapter, and understanding this takes some time and thought, both of which are at a premium these days. Having said that, Stoicism is currently mainstream enough to be worthy of some myth busting.

So, let's jump right in and take a look at some of the most common myths around the philosophy.

Suppressing Emotions

A common misperception upon reading Stoicism is that emotions are somehow invalid and that all emotion is nothing compared to the ideal that is rationality. The Stoics don't make any allusion to emotions when talking of virtue and rationality; reason and the like are what prevail.

To be fair, the ancient Stoics don't do a great job of clarifying the role of emotions. Or perhaps they did, and these texts are lost to time. Either way, the truth is that Stoicism isn't about the negation of emotions. If anything, it is the incorporation of them alongside the logical framework to arrive at a rational decision.

Consider Epictetus' story about the Stoic teacher who was aboard a sinking ship. There is no doubt that the emotions he felt during this moment were valid. After all, how could they not be. You see, Stoicism isn't about behaving like a robot. It is about trying to place your emotions in the right perspective and then using them to instruct your way forward.

When emotions are used alongside logic, a rational path appears. So, what is the Stoic way of handling emotions? Well, the trick is to not identify with them and recognize their ability to exaggerate and turn things into referendums about yourself.

Every Stoic principle is really about avoiding this mistake. This is why we remind ourselves of how small we are and how things don't matter anywhere near as much as we think they do. All of this is to avoid having the emotion-based ego take over and corrupt our path toward virtue.

Furthermore, when we identify and attach ourselves with our emotions, we remove all traces of objectivity from our decision-making patterns. In such a state, we cannot be expected to act in a manner which is beneficial to both ourselves and society. The true Stoic acknowledges emotions as being valid and existing for a reason. Once this is done, the Stoic redirects emotions toward assisting them and remaining wary of the ability of negative emotions' power to enslave a person.

Truth be told, there is valid criticism of the Stoic method of handling emotion. In terms of effectiveness, this is an easier said than done method which a lot of people will have trouble implementing, and one of the ways they'll do this is by simply ignore all emotions. This is contrary to Stoic belief, but neither does the belief provide a practical way of handling this situation.

In contrast, Buddhist philosophy provides a far better framework. A good way to think of Buddhism is to look at it as the sum of Stoicism along with emotional intelligence appended to it.

Acceptance

The Stoic message of accepting reality and aligning oneself with it causes a lot of misinterpretations. The most common question asked in response to this tenet is to ask whether or not a Stoic would simply accept tyranny perpetrated against them. To answer this question, we need to go back a bit and examine the basic principles of the philosophy.

Stoicism is not a passive philosophy for living. If anything, it is one of the most active methods of living, as I've illustrated previously. Stoic thought believes in accepting reality only in order to help you get your mind geared toward peace and clarity as much as possible. It is only from this place that you can make rational decisions.

A rational decision could very well involve revolution. There is nothing in Stoicism that talks about accepting things passively. Every event has to be analyzed in a rational manner. In order to do this, you need to first accept that the event exists and that you are in the situation.

Without this acceptance, how could you resist giving into your negative emotions? When a crime or injustice has been perpetrated against us, negative emotion is natural. Should we then lash out in response to the negative emotion, or should we seek to nullify it through rational action?

The Stoic choice is clear. This is why Stoicism always emphasizes the point that a philosopher needs to live their philosophy. Merely talking about it is not enough. Action is emphasized every step of the way, and to not take action against injustice is to behave irrationally and not practice Stoic philosophy.

Thus, passive resignation being a Stoic method of dealing with things is a myth and is, in fact, the exact opposite of Stoic belief. The aim is to accept reality, and if it isn't to your liking, take action to change it so that it turns to your liking, focusing on the process the whole way.

Hedonistic Tendencies

With all of this focus on being present and on ignoring the past or the future, does Stoicism imply that we should live only for the present moment? This misconception is easy to believe, and it is a fair one too because Hedonism existed as a smaller subculture during the time of Zeno.

Hedonism was simply an amalgamation of the Cynic philosophy of nothing mattering and the Epicurean belief system of happiness being the ultimate goal of life ("A Quick History of Philosophy," 2019). Needless to say, the Hedonist belief system is an unsustainable one since the focus on short-term pleasure at the expense of long-term gain is to simply adopt an imbalanced view of things.

There was a lot of this "the present moment is the best moment" stuff floating around back then, so it's natural that Stoic philosophy contains it as well. What is different is the context around which the Stoics frame the present moment. The carpe diem-type of lifestyle (YOLO for millennials) emphasizes that life is short and that one needs to seize the day and really squeeze the juice out of it. So, go out and do everything you wish.

Personally, I find it tough to understand how someone who spends even five minutes reading Stoic thought can arrive at such a misconception, but here we are anyway. As Seneca clarifies, it isn't so much that people's lives are short. It's just that people tend to waste far too much time in their lives on things that don't matter (Oppong, 2017).

When viewed this way, the other principles of focusing on things you can control, ignoring the externals, minimizing the identification with emotions and so on all make sense. Seneca further circles out the practice of "heedless luxury" as being one of the prime-time wasters of life.

Therefore, the message is quite clear. Spend your time doing things which really matter. These things are actions which bring you toward virtue as defined by the four pillars, and exercise your judgment using as much rationality as is available to you without dismissing your emotions.

Again, Buddhist philosophy and Ancient Hindu philosophy do a far better job of clarifying this point than Stoicism does. Perhaps the fact that a lot of Stoic texts are lost to time plays a role in such obscurity. Either way, my point is that Stoicism is not alone in proposing such beliefs. Ultimately, the differences between ancient philosophies often comes down to the minute details. All of them tend to agree with one another on the broad strokes.

Pessimism

All right, we've reached the big one! Along with the suppression of emotions, this point gets a lot of airtime. After all, one of the Stoic practices I listed out in the second chapter had you actively visualizing the worst. What could be more pessimistic than that?

There's a huge difference between visualizing the worst with an anxious mind because you're afraid it will happen and visualizing it as a defensive mechanism to prevent yourself from being caught with your pants down if the situation arises. The intent behind both sets of visualizations is completely different.

The Stoic practice of visualizing the worst is merely a case of defensive pessimism. There is no doubt that optimism helps us perform better and helps us lead better lives. Research backs this up in spades (Silva, 2017). The glass half-full crowd not only enjoys greater happiness but also greater success in life when compared to the glass half-empty bunch.

However, there is a point beyond which optimism fails us. To understand this, let's look at when optimism helps us. When we set out on a task or a goal that we're not quite sure how we're going to achieve, it is optimism that keeps the fires lit as we seek out solutions. Once a solution is fleshed out, we begin to take action.

As we take action, we receive feedback as to whether we're doing things correctly or poorly, and the more feedback we receive the more corrections we need to make. It is here, in dealing with the small picture, that defensive pessimism helps us. When faced with a trip across the country, simply jumping into the car and telling your partner "I'm optimistic we'll make it!" is a surefire way to sleeping on the couch for the rest of your life.

Instead, adopting a defensively pessimistic mindset by envisioning the things that could go wrong will help you prepare better with regard to the details. Are your maps ready to go? Do you have a backup in case the battery dies? Packed your toothbrush? Is there enough gas in the tank? Do you have enough money to pay for gas? Where will you stay along the way if this is a multi-day trip? If you're taking medication, is everything good to go there?

Asking such questions is just common sense and we do it all the time, but when the Stoics propose this exact same thing, everyone starts yelling "pessimism!" The key is knowing when and how to apply it. Optimism applied to the big picture works. You're optimistic you'll get there. I mean, why wouldn't you be?

When it comes to fleshing out the details, that is the process of getting there, defensive pessimism works best. The reserve clause is also meant by design to protect you from running away with your own optimism, which people can do. It's all about staying in the middle and remaining balanced by recognizing reality.

When it comes to goal setting, people talk optimism but often practice the exact opposite of the process I just described. They worry incessantly about reaching their goals and about how long it takes to get there. They worry about whether it'll be worth it when they get there or not. What will others think of them when they get there and so on.

Yet, when it comes to doing the work, they act in haphazard ways and don't pay attention to the details or feedback. All negative feedback is simply dismissed as coming from "haterz" and they plod on, optimistic as ever ("I wear sunglasses all the time coz my future is so bright, bro!"). This is why most people don't reach their goals and bounce from one seminar to the next like a bunch of self-improvement junkies.

Stoicism provides a clear path and framework to think about your life and goals while elegantly illustrating the way the world really is. There are things outside of your control, so hope for the best that they work out in your favor. If they don't, oh well, there's nothing you can do about it. This is the optimistic bit.

When it comes to the details of the process though, you are in full control. You should ensure that you execute everything you can to the best of your abilities and nothing less. This involves constant introspection. Are you doing the best that you can? What were the mistakes you made? Where can you improve? Have you taken care of everything you can take care of? This is the pessimistic bit.

Hopefully you can see the differences and the misinterpretation that gives rise to this erroneous belief that Stoics are a pessimistic bunch. Sure, they're not a bunch of unicorns bouncing around in a field, but Stoic philosophy can hardly be said to be pessimistic.

Stoics Are an Annoying Bunch!

I won't deny that the constant stream of articles from some wannapreneur boasting about how Stoicism helped him secure series A funding for his cute little startup gets to me as well. The fact is that the startup business world lends itself very well to the adoption of Stoic practices.

If you think about it, a startup is constantly fighting fires and needs to solve problems quickly. Their future is uncertain, and the ground is always shifting. Lastly, it is just so damn hard! No wonder a Stoic framework provides a great way for founders and high-level CEOs to operate within.

Despite the growing number of Instagram models highlighting the benefits of Stoic coffee with their morning Yoga, I'd like to point out that Stoic philosophy is not about talking as much as it is about doing. Right from the beginning, Zeno always spoke about the importance of doing over simply talking.

This is why there isn't too much academic discussion of Stoic thought, and the only academic contributions have appeared recently analyzing the applicability of Stoicism to modern life (Holiday, 2018). There are no five-volume tomes of 10,000 pages each talking about Stoicism. The message is clear: go out and do it!

As a final word, if anyone brags about how awesomely Stoic they are, I mean, do they even Stoic, bro?

Valid Criticism

A true book about Stoicism would be incomplete without including a section highlighting how Stoicism is not the be all and end all of philosophy. Yes, it is a great framework, but life is far too complex to be simply described by a single philosophy. Ironically, Stoicism attempts to do a good job of addressing the naysayers but gets too caught up with itself to actually iron out flaws.

A good example of this is the Stoic assumption that people always act in their own best interest. This is the same belief one would find in Cynical texts as well, and is in fact the foundation upon which modern economics is built. Either way, Stoicism assumes the worst about people but then gets twisted trying to explain the approach to behaving with such people.

The Stoic view is that such people are misguided in their beliefs and that if their beliefs are contrary to the greater good, then they are wrong. It is always the utilitarian Stoic who remains right. I've introduced the word utilitarian on purpose here to highlight the deficiencies of this thought process. No one needs to be told the fallacy of thinking that the majority is always right, and the minority should sacrifice their needs to the majority every single time. While normative ethics makes it very clear that it is an academic model and not a fully practical one, Stoicism doesn't present itself in this manner.

Stoicism thus doesn't concern itself with whether the Stoic himself has a less than complete picture of things. In all fairness, a lot of Stoic work on logic and deduction is not available, and modern Stoicism simply deduces what this framework might have been by inference from other works. Chrysippus would have definitely had a lot to say about all of this but we simply don't know what he really thought (Robertson, 2018).

It therefore becomes easy for a Stoic to adopt a fundamentalist view with regard to a lot of things. The only safeguard against this is to heed Marcus' warning to remind oneself of his or her mortality constantly.

Another very valid criticism of Stoic philosophy is that it doesn't provide a useful framework when it comes to handling emotions. I've touched on this before in previous chapters as well, but let's take a deeper look at it. You see, the Stoics tend to handle emotions as being something close to invalid. Their validity only exists in that they're meant to be supplanted by rationality.

I'm going to directly quote Marcus here. See what you make of this point of view (Carvajal, 2016):

Just as when meat or other foods are set before us we think, this is a dead fish, a dead bird or pig; and also, this fine wine is only the juice of a bunch of grapes, this purple-edged robe just sheep's wool dyed in a bit of blood from a shellfish; or of sex, that it is only rubbing private parts together followed by a spasmic discharge—in the same way our impressions grab actual events and permeate them, so we see them as they really are. —Marcus Aurelius

Dead fish, dead bird, bunch of grapes, sheep's wool, rubbing of private parts...all right, that's going over the line! This whole business of seeing things as they really are involved the removal of emotion completely, and a lot of Stoic believers these days gloss over this fact when selling Stoicism to the masses.

Modern Stoicism fails to address how or even why emotions are meant to be inferior to rationality. While it's true that emotions cause us to carry out ill-informed actions, the same can be said about robotic rationality as well. Consider the questions being posed by the rise of AI these days. Let me use an example to highlight this.

Microsoft developed an AI chatbot named Tay and unleashed it to the masses. Things went well right up until the point Tay began denying the genocide and blaming the world's woes on Muslims and immigrants (Vincent, 2016). It was pulled immediately, and Microsoft quietly binned the whole thing.

Tay had only rationality at its disposal. AI is therefore the ultimate Stoic, always utilitarian.

Does this mean Tay's actions were virtuous? All there is is silence from the Stoic crowd.

As an epilogue to this story, in case you're wondering, yes, of course Taylor Swift sued Microsoft for this stunt.

Chapter 9: Simple Daily Regimen for the Modern Stoic

Stoicism is all about doing stuff. With this in mind, it makes perfect sense to practice exercises which will help you develop a Stoic view of the world. These exercises have been collected from various Stoic texts, with most of them being prescribed by our three famous philosophers: Seneca, Marcus Aurelius, and Epictetus.

I've divided these into sections pertaining to the ideal time of day they need to be practiced. Ideal in this sense means to practice them at the time recommended by these scholars. If you find that a particular practice makes more sense for you later in the day or at some other time, go for it. The idea is to make things as easily repeatable for you as possible.

There are a large number of exercises provided here. Start off with a few and then expand as you get used to them. So, let's now look at some morning exercises you can do which will get your day started off right.

Morning Exercises

These exercises are best performed at the start of your day. If you have an irregular schedule, this means you ought to perform these right after you wake up, whenever that is. There are some exercises which call for a morning walk or contemplation in nature. If possible, do these in the hours of dawn as the sun rises since the environment at that time of the day differs from the rest.

Meditation

Given the intersection between Buddhism and Stoicism, it should come as no surprise that meditation makes the list. While different from the Buddhist technique, the aim of Stoic meditation is the same. Withdraw into yourself upon waking up and take a mental note of everything that is within you. The idea is to observe yourself in a calm and detached manner.

It is important to spend some time by yourself during these hours. Exercises such as observing your breath or even walking in nature and contemplating the stars and the rising sun are great ways to reflect on the nature of things. This might sound a bit highbrow, but take the time to reflect on your place in nature. Adopt Plato's view as described before and note the significance (or lack thereof) of your problems when in nature.

If walking in nature is not accessible to you at this time, journey inward and spend some time observing yourself.

Rehearsal

As you contemplate, bring your awareness to the general principles of Stoicism. Think of these as the overarching themes of your life. For example, remind yourself of the fact that nothing is certain and that a lot of things are outside your control. Rehearse the general precepts of Stoicism in your mind.

Next, move your attention to the tasks that lie ahead of you that day. Make your plans using inputs from the previous day's reflection and use them to inform your actions. Remember to remind yourself that while your intention may be one thing and that you might want a particular result, something outside your control might derail your efforts.

So, give yourself the luxury of the reserve clause while taking care to avoid using this as an excuse to shirk responsibility. When reminding yourself of the fact that things could go wrong, keep in mind that you still wish to act a certain way. Remind yourself of what these qualities are and see yourself behaving in that manner when something is denied to you.

Once in a while, contemplate how uncertain things are due to the fact that nothing is in your control. This makes it even more crucial that you focus on the present and let the past lie where it belongs.

What Would X Do?

Once in a while try asking yourself what your philosophical ideal would do. This is a very powerful exercise since it forces you to think in a frame of mind outside of your own, even if you don't have the full picture of how someone else would act. The point is to force yourself to view things from an outside perspective.

When contemplating the day's tasks, ask yourself how your ideal philosopher would deal with them and what would they do when a favorable result was denied to them. In fact, this is a good practice, not just for the morning but for the entire day.

Daytime Exercises

Daytime here refers to your regular workday and all the time you spend between wakefulness and preparing for sleep. So, don't think of these exercises as ending when the sun sets. Ancient Greek life used to pretty much wind up once the sun set, which is why you'll find a lot of those texts referring to these as daytime or to the time when light was available.

Prosoche

Prosoche can be roughly translated as what we think of as mindfulness, but it is a more intellectual and rationally focused pursuit than the Buddhist practice. Think of it as being Stoic mindfulness. This calls for you to exercise those qualities of yours which enhance your virtue in a given situation.

Keep your awareness on the task in front of you but never lose sight of the ultimate aim in life, which is to travel along the path of virtue. Are your actions in line with the pillars of virtue? If so, keep going. Always contemplate and be aware of your actions and especially your words when interacting with others.

When externals sabotage your plans, remember to return to your pillars of virtue and practice Stoic reframing. This means view every incident in your life, good or bad, as being another opportunity to practice Stoic thought. Always be on guard for your mind being corrupted by your own foolish actions and carelessness.

Acceptance

This exercise really amounts to practicing equanimity. When any external forces you off the path of virtue, bring yourself back by reminding yourself that equanimity and acceptance are ideal states of mind. Reframe the situation and remind yourself that you wished for this and that you are in control of your own actions and reactions to events.

Heed the Stoic teaching of wishing for everything that has occurred to occur in exactly the way it has and to not wish for something else. If you do this, you will be able to focus your mind on the solutions a lot faster. Recognize that externals or indifferents do not matter one bit to your happiness.

Lusiteles

The Stoics recommended viewing everything in life as involving a series of transactions. For everything that occurs in your life, you pay via an action conducted by yourself. Investing your actions entirely towards an indifferent is unlikely to bring you much profit (lusiteles).

Instead, actions invested towards virtue bring you peace of mind and greater profit thanks to the fact that virtue is a reward all by itself. Hence, in any situation, ask yourself what it is you're investing and what you're getting back as a reward. Often, life will demand payment in the form of inflicting externals onto you.

This payment is simply for the privilege of keeping your sanity intact. This is what life demands as payment, and when viewed this way, the occasional damaging external doesn't seem too bad a price to pay.

Distance and Delay

The Stoic placed a great deal of emphasis on not identifying emotionally with occurrences in your life. This applies equally to good as well as bad situations. If any hugely attractive situation manifests itself, enjoy it but remember that nothing lasts forever and that the results are an indifferent.

Similarly, behave in the same manner when a negative happens. Wherever there's an opportunity to learn from something, do so, but always keep in mind that the path of virtue is what's most important. Wherever possible, delay your response to events. For example, if something good happens or you're close to achieving it or taking actions towards it, ask yourself, "What are the negatives in the situation?"

View both the positive and negative side of things before committing to an action. Enforcing a delay gives you time to evaluate your actions as well as remove the influence of the emotions of the present moment. This way you'll behave in as rational a manner as possible. Another technique you can employ is to ask yourself what this event would look like if it happened to someone else?

What would your reaction be when observing this happening to someone else? For example, if you have just lost a loved one, as difficult as dealing with it is, ask yourself what you would tell someone else who had just lost their loved one. Probably that this is an unavoidable part of life and that death happens. Grieve, but don't lose yourself in it. Use this point of view to inform your own behavior towards events.

Suspend Judgment

There are two parts to this practice. First, if someone carries out actions that are punitive towards your, then delay judging this person. Remind yourself that this person was acting out of their own perception of reality and, in their mind, what they're doing is the right thing. In other words, they simply don't know better.

To spend your time castigating this person as good or bad is to take yourself out of the actions required to achieve virtue, so prize that above all else. This goes back to the point made just now about the importance of distancing and delaying your reactions to things.

The second portion of this practice deals with hearsay. When you hear someone else speaking of the actions of a third person, suspend your judgment. First, ask yourself to what degree those actions affect your life. If they do, follow the first point. If they don't, why bother with them?

As a practical example, the daily ins and outs of politics affect people's emotional states quite a lot. However, the practical effects of these so-called political "debates" don't mean a thing in the long run. Learn to discern what is truly important by avoiding the rush to judgment.

Train Yourself

Epictetus advises everyone to constantly be training themselves in self-discipline and their psychological state. Self-discipline entails practicing and sticking to a routine as well as following the Stoic precepts. Psychological toughness involves a lot of things which can be boiled down to "push your limits."

He uses crazy sounding examples such as withholding water in your mouth when you're really thirsty to delaying your intake of food a little bit every time you're hungry. In reality, these examples are probably his way of exhorting people to curb their instincts for instant gratification, which is now more important than ever.

When training yourself, train your body but place a higher importance on training your mind and will. Practice letting go of your need for things to happen a certain way and be comfortable with visualizing the exact opposite happening. This doesn't mean you should wish for it, but keep the thought in mind and remind yourself that no matter what happens, you'll be perfectly fine and able to cope with it.

After all, the results you achieve are externals and it is the process that matters the most. So, always practice on focusing your thoughts on the process in the moment. When your mind drifts towards the perspective that good results "need" to happen, pull yourself back to reality and virtue by following Stoic practices.

Flip the Script

This is simply the Stoic practice of inversion in action. Every obstacle is an opportunity and every loss is you simply giving back something that was loaned to you in the first place. For example, youth is not lost but is simply given back to the Gods who loaned it to you.

Reflect on how everything is impermanent and develop greater realization of this through your meditation. Once you realize this, you'll come to see that everything in your life has been loaned to you. Nothing is truly "yours." Upon death, you need to give everything back.

Keep this in mind when you lose something and also remind yourself of this during the day. When you do this, you'll realize how valuable your time is and how little of it you're actually maximizing.

Act for the Sake of It

Remember always that the process and what you control is the path to wisdom and happiness (virtue). The results are externals. In addition to this, when you make your plans, keep in mind the importance of the reserve clause.

Do not use the reserve clause to shirk responsibility as the unwise would. Instead, use it to remind yourself of the relative importance of things and of your place in the grand scheme of things.

Philostorgia

This practice might be a bit difficult for some since it goes back to the valid criticisms of Stoicism I discussed in the previous chapter. Either way, wish good upon your enemies and always keep in mind that they do not know any better. Contemplate both their actions and the actions of those you admire and ask yourself what thought process and assumptions underlie such behavior.

Always seek to give back to mankind and love all men. Everyone comes from the same source, so to wish ill upon someone is to wish ill upon yourself. Act with as much decisiveness as you can muster and with the correct intentions. If fate wills it, you will realize the fruit of your actions. If not, so be it.

Oikeiosis

This practice is in combination with the previous one. Visualize yourself and your existence as being a tiny dot in the entire chain of the cosmos. Remind yourself of how vast the universe is and how long it has existed before you and how long it will exist once you leave this life.

The entire existence of the universe, including this world's, is a chain of events, and you're a part of it as is everyone else around you. All of you are created from the same thing and are like individual cells of a larger organism. So, act with kindness and benevolence and remind yourself of the principles of virtue at all times.

Nighttime Exercises

As your day draws to a close, take some time to contemplate and meditate upon how you spent your day. This is the best time to journal, and the practice of the evening meditation will help guide you with regard to what you need to record.

Evening Meditation

Review the day from start to finish three times before journaling. As you do so, ask yourself the following questions:

1. What did you do wrong?

2. What did you do right in accordance with virtue?

3. What could have been done better, outside your mistakes?

The objective is not to get emotionally involved with these points but to instead adopt a detached third-person view of things. Imagine yourself as a doctor, diagnosing a patient. Your focus is on the problem and developing a diagnosis, not with worrying about how terribly you behaved and how bad your failings and shortcomings are.

When asking yourself what you did wrong, do so with a view to evaluating yourself from the perspective of virtue, not results. Praise yourself for behaving in line with virtue when evaluating what you did well. If there's nothing you can find in this point, look harder. Even the smallest action is noteworthy, and this is why it is important to evaluate your day three times.

There are always things you can improve. The things you did wrong are an obvious starting point. However, examine your good moments as well to see if there's anything else you could have done.

Relaxation

When adopting the intention to relax, it is important to actually do so. Many people use the initial moments of sleep to go over their day and plan ahead and so on. Do not do this. Even when relaxing, it is important to be fully present and to allow your mind to let go of whatever is agitating it.

Always complete your evening meditation thoroughly since this will give you the attitude of having done everything you possibly could during that day. Seneca clarifies this by saying that if you were to die overnight, you would do so in the most content manner possible. The practice of evening meditation achieves this along with your action of letting go of the events of the day.

Chapter 10: Stoic Lessons for a Modern Leader

There has never been a shortage of leaders and those willing to thrust themselves into positions from where they can command people. Often, these people seek such positions because of the power inherent in them instead of trying to adopt such positions for the sake of carrying out the work necessary.

In other words, it isn't the virtue of the position that is important to such people but the power that it commands. However, things are not so bleak. Just as there have been people who have sought power, there have always been an equal number of people who have simply sought to execute what is in front of them.

In this chapter, we're going to look at examples of leadership from an Ancient Roman statesman, a President of the United States, a Super Bowl-winning football coach, and a billionaire. If you're in a position of leadership or seek such a position, paying heed to the lessons from the stories of these people will be extremely beneficial for you.

First, let's travel all the way back to the dying days of the Roman Empire.

Cato the Younger

There is always the danger of reading far too much into the lives of people long since dead, from times which are not relevant anymore. I say this because it becomes far too easy to either cherry pick the good things or highlight just the bad.

Thus, objectivity becomes difficult to achieve. In a book of this size, it is not possible to fully recount each and every event in a person's life.

Having said that, since our objective is to understand the tenets of Stoicism through the lens of leadership, we can draw objective lessons from Cato the Younger's life. Cato, who would be granted the honorific Uticensis after his death, is often held up as a shining example of incorruptibility during a time when the Roman Empire was suffering from a bout of corruption that would ultimately lead to Julius Caesar crowning himself dictator and bringing an end to an era.

From a young age, Cato displayed a stubbornness that earned him the respect of his peers ("Inspiring Examples of Stoic Leadership - How Cato Lives On 2000 Years Later - What Is Stoicism?" 2018). He grew up an orphan, but was raised in an extremely wealthy household. Like all Roman boys hailing from wealthy backgrounds, Cato was well-versed in the art of war and rhetoric. His natural path took him into the halls of government, and this is where he began to fulfill the promise he had always shown since his childhood.

Cato is particularly known for displaying a streak of fairness and his unwillingness to get caught up with the luxuries of his position, something Marcus would imitate many years later. As a military leader, Cato was one of the better Roman generals, but what really stands out about him is his willingness to partake in the hardships his men endured.

As the most powerful fighting force in the ancient world, the Roman military was no cakewalk for the average legionnaire ("Inspiring Examples of Stoic Leadership - How Cato Lives On 2000 Years Later - What Is Stoicism?" 2018). However, as his men first set eyes on their new commander, they saw a plainly dressed man walking into camp instead of riding on horseback accompanied by an entourage.

His reputation had preceded him, so they understood that Cato was not a political climber looking to sacrifice lives in order to further his political goals. This was someone who ate last, drank last, and ensured the spoils of war were properly divided before partaking in them ("Inspiring Examples of Stoic Leadership - How Cato Lives On 2000 Years Later - What Is Stoicism?" 2018). His willingness to share their hardship engendered loyalty among his legions that went beyond words.

Cato is best known for his staunch opposition to Caesar's attempts to grab power. As a quaestor, Cato is well known for auditing and prosecuting tax collectors involved in accepting bribes and advocating prison terms for those involved in corruption. This was an exemplary attitude for a senator to exhibit at a time when such things were considered routine.

Despite being physically abused by Caesar's supporters and constantly harassed, Cato never stopped his opposition to what he saw as a destructive power grab by the former. He repeatedly blocked laws and introduced reforms which made it harder for Caesar to usurp power. In doing this, Cato placed himself up against possibly the three most powerful men in the world at the time: Caesar, Pompey, and Marcus Crassus, who was the wealthiest man in the world (and is in fact the wealthiest man to have ever lived).

Cato's opposition to Caesar eventually found its way to the battlefield and came to a head at Utica. Upon suffering defeat, Cato committed suicide, unable to bear the thought of having to face a victorious Caesar or even worse, being pardoned by him. The honorific Uticensis was later bestowed upon him for this act.

The appending of such terms was usually reserved for those generals who won a great victory. Cato is perhaps the only Roman general to be awarded this honor in defeat, such was his reputation.

Cato might have lost the battle, but it's safe to say he won the war against Caesar. Viewed from a Stoic perspective, Cato is the one who lived well and died honorably, as opposed to being stabbed to death by the people he trusted the most, like Caesar.

Teddy Roosevelt

The first Roosevelt to serve as president is more myth than man at this point. His life serves as great instruction in not just Stoicism but many other things. Roosevelt was born into a wealthy family in New York, and most of his family members would eventually find their way into business.

As a child he suffered from severe asthmatic attacks which caused the sensation of being suffocated to death. There was no cure for his affliction, but young Teddy embarked on a regime of intense physical activity whenever he could find the time. A naturally curious child, he showed great interest in nature and even established a rudimentary "Roosevelt Museum of Natural History" as a kid where he would display stuffed animals (Holiday, 2019).

The Roosevelt family traveled abroad quite a lot, and this helped Teddy form cosmopolitan world views at a young age. Furthermore, he learned from the lessons life taught him every step of the way. After being bullied by two boys in camp, he decided to strengthen himself physically and took up boxing lessons with gusto.

Roosevelt later credited his father with being the biggest influence on his life. He said that his father combined strength with tolerance and gentleness and had no patience for dishonesty, idleness or cowardice of any sort. Upon entering Harvard College, Teddy's father advised him to look after his morals first, then his health, and then finally his studies.

It seems astounding to consider this, but the younger Roosevelt was already a renowned ornithologist by the time he had entered Harvard. His interest in nature led him to publish a lengthy book about the birds present in upstate New York, and he somehow managed to balance working on this book with his heavy academic coursework.

He graduated near the top of his class and soon married Alice Lee. Unfortunately, two days after the birth of their daughter, Alice passed away. This led Roosevelt to famously note in his journal that the light had gone out of his life. Further compounding his woe was that his mother had also passed away a few hours earlier (Holiday, 2019).

Following this, Roosevelt threw himself wholeheartedly into politics and government life. Although people remember him as being one of America's greatest presidents, Roosevelt made an equally strong mark as the commissioner of the New York City Police Department.

Following the publication of a book that detailed the hell that the city's new immigrants were forced through, Roosevelt accompanied the writer through the troubled neighborhoods around Mulberry Street in Manhattan, which prompted the writer Jacob Riis to note the following (Riis, 2008):

When Roosevelt read [my] book, he came... No one ever helped as he did. For two years we were brothers in (New York City's crime-ridden) Mulberry Street. When he left, I had seen its golden age... There is very little ease where Theodore Roosevelt leads, as we all of us found out. The lawbreaker found it out who predicted scornfully that he would "knuckle down to politics the way they all did" and lived to respect him, though he swore at him, as the one of them all who was stronger than pull... That was what made the age golden, that for the first time a moral purpose came into the street. In the light of it everything was transformed.

Roosevelt faced resistance during his time as commissioner. In one instance he was invited to a demonstration which was aimed at protesting against his policies. This invite was extended in jest since the aim was to insult Roosevelt. However, not only did Roosevelt attend, but he also laughed at the insults thrown his way. Ironically, the people attending left with a better impression of him than they arrived with.

The most storied act of Roosevelt's life was when he was shot at point blank range by a fanatic when running for president and miraculously survived thanks to the long sheaf of notes that were his speech. Upon his staff trying to rush him to the hospital, he famously quipped that it would take more than that to kill a Bull Moose (which was the name of his party, naturally).

Teddy Roosevelt is the embodiment of amor fati. He lived for challenges and dealt with his troubles Stoically. This is not a coincidence since he always carried with him a copy of the discourses of Epictetus (Riis, 2008).

Amancio Ortega

Who, you might be wondering, was Amacio Ortega? Ortega happens to be the owner of Inditex, which is a retail chain that owns the brands Zara, Pull and Bear, and Massimo Dutti, amongst others. He is also one of the richest people in the world, and at one point was the second richest person on the planet with a net worth of close to $70 billion (Marlow, 2017).

Not that any of that matters to this eighty-something-year-old. Born in 1936 in northern Spain after the Spanish Civil War, Ortega grew up in a poor family. His father was a railroad worker and his mother was a housemaid. Growing up, he came to terms with the fact that everyone in the family needed to make money and produce something.

With this in mind, he began working in a clothing shop at the age of thirteen, and by the age of twenty, he, his siblings, and his future wife, Rosalia Mera, were making women's bathrobes out of a small shop. Progress was slow but in 1975, they opened their first store and added stores to their portfolio slowly but steadily.

All this hard work paid off handsomely as Ortega and Mera's work methods revolutionized the retail industry. Zara became famous for its quick stock turnovers which kept shoppers coming back for more, and they pioneered a retail distribution system which is still unmatched in the industry.

Ortega has done all of this with minimal outside investment, and he still owns close to sixty percent of his company. So, how does the now eighty-something Ortega spend his time? Well, he lives on a farm which is ten miles away from the headquarters of Inditex and raises chickens. He still travels the ten miles or so to the office and eats lunch in the company cafeteria with the rest of his workers.

Astonishingly, he doesn't wear a stitch of Zara's clothes, preferring a simple button-down shirt and a navy blazer with slacks. For a man who is a founder of one of the most fashionable brands in the world, he doesn't really care for fashion. He still visits the same coffee shop he has visited over the years and still lives in northern Spain where he has spent most of his life.

Is he a Stoic? We don't know since he doesn't speak all that much. However, in an age when people love flaunting their cash on social media and new age gurus showcase their private jets and market themselves as being bosses in a Bentley, here is a man who doesn't care for all of that and clearly embodies a lot of Stoic principles.

Pete Carroll

Football fans will recognize this name, but for those who don't, Pete Carroll is one of the greatest college football coaches of all time and is also a Super Bowl-winning coach with the Seattle Seahawks. As of this writing, he is still the head coach, having occupied the position for close to a decade, and is one of the longest-tenured coaches in a notoriously impatient league (Babb, 2019).

Carroll is famously known for being optimistic and upbeat, much to the amusement of the press corps that follows him. As a kid, he dreamed of playing football professionally, but his physical abilities didn't lend themselves very well to the sport. However, despite weighing in at only 150 pounds, he managed to become a multi-sport star in high school and even played college football at the University of the Pacific.

Following graduation, he tried out for a pro spot but didn't make it. Faced with real-life bills, he began selling roofing materials as a salesman, but this frustrated him even more. He sought a job as a collegiate assistant coach and soon found a job as a graduate assistant at Pacific.

Thus began a meandering career which would eventually take him into the NFL as a positions coach and later to a coordinator level. By all accounts, Carroll was very good at his job and was appointed the head coach of an NFL team in 1994. Unfortunately, this team happened to be the New York Jets, and following a losing season, he was immediately fired.

He was subsequently selected to replace the legendary Bill Parcells at New England, but with a creditable win/loss record and a lack of management support, he was fired when Robert Kraft bought the team in 1999. His overall record in the NFL was 33-31 and he was burnt out.

Carroll spent the next year as a consultant and even moonlighted as a writer for Sports Illustrated, but despite offers to coach as a coordinator, he never took them up. Meanwhile, the once legendary University of Southern California Trojans had hastily gotten rid of their coach after yet another terrible season. In what was a shock announcement, Carroll got the job.

If this were Hollywood, this is precisely where our hero would prove his doubters wrong. However, this was real life. USC duly stumbled its way to yet another abysmal season, prompting calls to fire the unsuccessful NFL coach who was the last choice as a hire for the team. Well, Carroll kept his job and a turnaround did come. Here is a list of what his teams achieved in the previous decade:

- Two national championship game appearances in 2005 and 2006, with the 2006 loss to Texas considered one of the greatest NCAA games of all time.

- AP national champions in 2003 and 2004.

- Seven consecutive AP top four finishes.

- 33 consecutive weeks as the top-ranked AP team, a national record.

- 34 game winning streak between 2003 to 2004.

- 53 players selected in the NFL draft, with 14 in the first round.

- An 83.6% winning record (97-19).

- Three Heisman Trophy winners.

USC was subsequently named the college football team of the decade by ESPN. Life wasn't done with Carroll though. A recruiting scandal followed which led to him being removed from his post, despite all the success he achieved, and it is at this point that he joined the Seahawks. When leaving USC, he was derided by one sportswriter as having gone from saint to scallywag, from the greatest to being the greatest embarrassment for USC (Babb, 2019).

In a turnaround of life situations, Carroll was now mocked as being the optimistic college football guy who couldn't cut it in the NFL. The trademark unimpressive Carroll seasons followed and by 2013 patience was wearing thin. A decent start was followed by a trip to the playoffs. Following a tight conference championship game, Carroll's team were heavy underdogs in the Super Bowl. They blew Denver away 43-8 securing Seattle's first ever Super Bowl win.

The following year, Seattle bossed the league and went into a second consecutive Super Bowl, this time against Carroll's old team, the Patriots. What followed continues to drive the media narrative around Carroll to this day. With the ball on the first yard line, Carroll made the fateful decision to throw the ball instead of running it in. The resultant interception gave New England the win and Carroll was hounded by the media as having bottled it once again.

Carroll simply moved on and remained positive. He was faced with the task of dismantling his team, the most successful team in franchise history, but has seen it through, nonetheless.

You might be wondering what is one of Carroll's favorite books? *The Obstacle is the Way* by noted modern Stoic, Ryan Holiday.

Conclusion

Stoicism continues to be one of the best philosophies to structure life around. The reason for this is its versatility, which is drawn from a wide variety of sources as you've seen throughout this book. While it isn't a comprehensive structure to guide your life, frankly, nothing ever is. So, this can hardly be counted as a shortcoming on Stoicism's part.

Having said that, there are some valid criticisms which are thrown its way and I've discussed these shortcomings in this book. While Stoicism can be accused of being a little blinkered with regards to its own logic, the fact is that a lot of our contemporary understanding of Stoicism comes from few sources, with the large majority being lost to time.

Despite that, the inherent wisdom shines through easily. The applicability of the philosophy from people as diverse as the ancient Greeks and Romans to leaders these days, the benefits of Stoicism are obvious. For leaders, Stoicism provides a handy template by which they can govern themselves and the people underneath them.

By doing do, not only does the Stoic inspire loyalty but actually ensures success for the most part. While it is true that success is never guaranteed, repeating a successful process over and over surely leads to some form of material success over a long period of time. This is the underpinning of all Stoic thought and is why the ancient Stoics emphasized focusing on the process instead of the reward.

The process itself is your reward and it is your focus on the process through the four pillars of virtue that will determine your progress along the path. Material results by themselves are preferred indifferents and while there's nothing wrong in chasing them, keep their relative importance in mind. This also will stop you from strangling your goals with worry about whether you'll achieve them or not.

A common pitfall is to assume that Stoicism dismisses all emotions as invalid and therefore the true Stoic is forever robotic and calculating. While it is true the Stoicism does not explain the role of emotions very well, this extreme view is hardly what is espoused. Instead of seeking to eliminate emotion, minimize its damage by not identifying with it and making it worse by building it to unseemly proportions within your head.

Above all else take care to avoid the misconceptions that have been listed in the relevant chapter in this book. Avoid trying to adopt the moral high ground and like Marcus advises, always be aware of your mortality and place in the grand scheme of things, which is another way of saying: you don't matter nearly as much as you like to think.

In a nutshell, this illustrates why misconceptions about Stoicism emerge. Either way, take the time to let the philosophy soak in and better yet, practice the routines and the qualities of the Stoic as discussed in this book. Adopting even a few of them, such as the morning and evening meditation, will go a long way to making your life a whole lot easier.

If you find yourself facing tough questions in your life, then do not hesitate to refer to the biographies and works of the philosophers quoted in this book. You'll find that Stoicism does have deep academic aspects to it, but the overwhelming importance placed on practicality results in a philosophy that is easily accessible to everybody.

To use a concept of the famous academic and author, Nassim Nicholas Taleb, Stoicism is antifragile. The more things go wrong in your life, the more relevant it becomes thanks to its ability to help you figure out what is relevant and what isn't. Examine your life through the good, bad and indifferent lenses and you'll find that your entire worldview is based on things that are ultimately irrelevant.

As Seneca said, human beings waste their time on a lot of things. Adopt Stoicism and watch as your life improves thanks to a better consciousness with regards to how your time is spent. Also, do not assume that everything that has been written about Stoicism is true and is gospel.

After all, the point of the philosophy is to live it. If you find something in your experience that contradicts the claims made in this book, and other Stoic texts, then feel free to adopt a counter viewpoint provided it is grounded in rationality. The Stoic decision-making process, or even the Platonian one, will guide you through the minefield of choices we often have to make in this regard.

Lastly, I hope you've found Stoicism as illuminating as I did when I first encountered it. Thank you for taking the time to read through this book. I hope reading it has been as much of a pleasure as writing it has been!

References

A Quick History of Philosophy. (2019). Retrieved from https://www.philosophybasics.com/general_quick_history.html

Anil, A. (2019). India and China Together can Lead the Fourth Industrial Revolution. Here's How | International | 2017-12-21 | web only. Retrieved from https://english.cw.com.tw/article/article.action?id=1771

Aptowicz, C. (2019). Could You Stomach the Horrors of 'Halftime' in Ancient Rome? Retrieved from https://www.livescience.com/53615-horrors-of-the-colosseum.html

Babb, K. (2019). Pete Carroll is the NFL's Oldest Head Coach. Retrieved from https://beta.washingtonpost.com/sports/2019/08/15/pete-carroll-is-nfls-oldest-head-coach-you-wouldnt-know-it-by-watching-him/

Carvajal, I. (2016). Debunking Some Myths About Stoicism - Micropreneur Life. Retrieved from https://micropreneur.life/debunking-some-myths-about-stoicism/

Gill, N. (2019). All About Roman Ruler Marcus Aurelius. Retrieved from https://www.thoughtco.com/who-was-marcus-aurelius-119719

Holiday, R. (2019). It's Going To Take More Than That To Stop You. Retrieved from https://dailystoic.com/its-going-to-take-more-than-that-to-stop-you/

Holiday, R. (2018). 12 Lessons On Leadership From The Last Great Emperor. Retrieved from https://dailystoic.com/12-lessons-on-leadership-from-the-last-great-emperor/

Inspiring Examples of Stoic Leadership - How Cato Lives On 2000 Years Later - What Is Stoicism? (2018). Retrieved from http://whatisstoicism.com/stoicism-resources/stoic-leadership/

Jacobi inversion problem. (2019). Retrieved from https://www.encyclopediaofmath.org/index.php/Jacobi_inversion_problem

Marcus Aurelius. (2019). Retrieved from https://www.historycrunch.com/marcus-aurelius.html#/

Marlow, B. (2017). The humble life of Zara owner Amancio Ortega is to be admired. Retrieved from https://www.telegraph.co.uk/finance/newsbysector/retailandconsumer/11656753/The-humble-life-of-Zara-owner-Amancio-Ortega-is-to-be-admired.html

Oppong, T. (2017). The Impediment to Action Advances Action. Retrieved from https://medium.com/personal-growth/the-impediment-to-action-advances-action-304ed19ef208

Pangloss-character. (2006). Retrieved from http://www.d-barfield.co.uk/Pangloss%20-%20Character.html

Pigliuci, M. (2016). Sophia vs Phronesis: two conceptions of wisdom. Retrieved from https://howtobeastoic.wordpress.com/2016/09/20/sophia-vs-phronesis-two-conceptions-of-wisdom/

Riis, J. (2008). *The making of an American*. Charleston, S.C.: BiblioBazaar.

Robertson, D. (2018). What do the Stoic Virtues Mean? Retrieved from https://donaldrobertson.name/2018/01/18/what-do-the-stoic-virtues-mean/

Salzberger, J. (2019). What Is Stoicism? A Simple Definition & 10 Stoic Core Principles. Retrieved from https://www.njlifehacks.com/what-is-stoicism-overview-definition-10-stoic-principles/#tab-con-1

Scott, E. (2018). What is Stoic Logic? Retrieved from https://ericsiggyscott.wordpress.com/2018/03/04/what-is-stoic-logic/

Silva, J. (2017). The Upside of Defensive Pessimism: The Potential Benefit Anxiety. Retrieved from https://positivepsychology.com/defensive-pessimism/

Song, A. (2019). Elon Musk: Humanity Is a Kind of 'Biological Boot Loader' for AI. Retrieved from https://www.wired.com/story/elon-musk-humanity-biological-boot-loader-ai/

Vincent, J. (2016). Twitter taught Microsoft's friendly AI chatbot to be a racist asshole in less than a day. Retrieved from https://www.theverge.com/2016/3/24/11297050/tay-microsoft-chatbot-racist

www.ingramcontent.com/pod-product-compliance
Lightning Source LLC
Chambersburg PA
CBHW030700220526
45463CB00005B/1850